William C. Pitt

Nineteen Months a Prisoner of War in the Hands of the Rebels

Experience at Belle Isle

William C. Pitt

Nineteen Months a Prisoner of War in the Hands of the Rebels
Experience at Belle Isle

ISBN/EAN: 9783337122720

Printed in Europe, USA, Canada, Australia, Japan

Cover: Foto ©ninafisch / pixelio.de

More available books at **www.hansebooks.com**

NINETEEN MONTHS

A PRISONER OF WAR

In the Hands of the Rebels:

EXPERIENCE AT BELLE ISLE,

RICHMOND, DANVILLE AND ANDERSONVILLE:

SOME ITEMS WITH REFERENCE TO

CAPT. WIRZ,

WITH A

MAP OF THE ANDERSONVILLE PRISON CAMP,
CALLED CAMP SUMTER.

MILWAUKEE:
STARR & SON, PRINTERS, 312 AND 314 EAST WATER STREET.
1865.

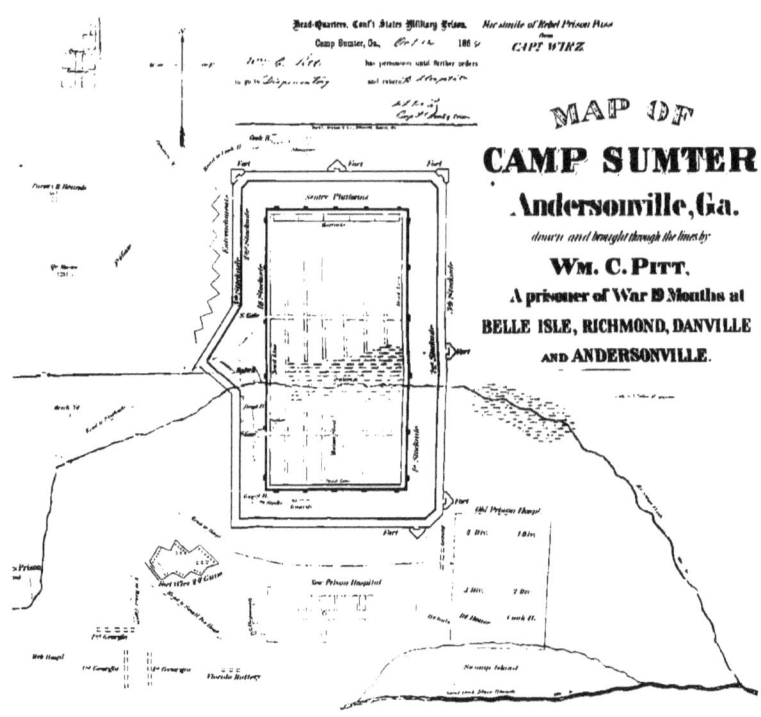

PREFACE.

What was intended only for a newspaper article in the outset, has resulted in the production of this work, growing out of the following circumstances: While writing the article above mentioned, the writer was introduced to Mr. Pitt, the author of the accompanying Map, who had also been a prisoner of war nineteen months, and at his urgent solicitation and for his benefit, the subject has been continued to its present proportions.

Writing in a hurry and having to keep ahead of proof, there will be many things, of course open to criticism, but if the author has contributed anything which will interest the public and aid a fellow soldier, he is amply compensated for his labor.

Chapter I.

THE WITCHES CAULDRON.

"Black Spirits and White,
Red Spirits, and Gray :
Mingle, mingle, mingle.
You that mingle, may."

The spirits who are described in the caption are not imaginary in the case of the late rebellion. They were real characters, and had their designs from the beginning of their political corner, each and every one of them. They were not so very great in numbers, but were in political influence, for the reason that men of talent could do a great deal better in any respectable business, than they could in any political office or position. In fact it has been notorious for a great many years that if a man accepted office, his honesty and integrity were at once a matter of *discussion* to say the least.

Without regard to party or professed principles that the office holders North and South have understood that they were elected for the purpose of pay and plunder, and the perpetuation of power in their own precious hands. It is not strange that these controlling men *soon* got into a wrangle among themselves, each one wanted to be leader, each one the largest quantity of the spoils. These spirits exactly alike in principle divided into antagonistic parties, and yet each one had the same object in view, namely to remove the bann of the Constitution and the laws which stood in the way of their plundering schemes and designs. It is not intended by the writer to say that every office holder of the government was influenced by the motives indicated above, but that a very great many *were*. Those who discharged their duties faithfully under the trying circumstances in which they were placed, are entitled to the honor, esteem and respect of every citizen of the United States. Of the planners and plotters of the overthrow of the Republic, no execration can be too great, no damnation too deep, whatever may have been their locality.

They were the "Black spirits" and it is too strongly suspected that they were to be found in all latitudes of this Republic at the breaking out of the war. They without hesitation plunged themselves into the witches cauldron, no doubt thinking that the witch being possessed of the devil like themselves would stir the pot in such a manner as to bring them out all right.

Another class, are those described above as discharging their duties faithfully under trying circumstances, men willing to sacrifice their all in what they believed to be right and for the good of their country. They went into the cauldron believing that right would bring them out all right, or at all events they were prepared for the *worst* in any emergency. The gray spirits being a mixture undecided in principles or opinions, went into the witches kettle in hopes that by the mixing, mingling and stirring they might bring themselves into some position in society which they knew well their talents or integrity did not entitle them to. When the witches wand was used, these heterogenous spirits did not mingle at all.

The red spirits who pretended to go into the cauldron, but did not—might be termed the Jacobins of the United States. They had no character or property to lose, but stood in the position of the man who wished that a passing steamer might blow up in order that he would be enabled to pick up some of the fragments of the wreck. They wanted war and blood, but never risked their carcases near a battle filed until the conflict was over and then they were the first to go and pick up the fragments.

They were of the character of the bloody triumviate of Robespierre, Murat and Dante, who could see the blood of their citizens by the guillotine floating through the streets of Paris, and pride themselves upon their success because it brought in one way and another money into their coffers.

Immediately after the election of Mr. Lincoln to the Presiidency—without any just cause, without any good motive, the "black spirits" of the South inaugurated the rebellion. There had never been a President of the United States more fairly elected than Mr. Lincoln. The Southern people had gone to the polls and voted against him, and of course must acknowledge the fairness of the contest. They had submitted their case to the ballot box, under the constitution and the laws, and they were concluded by it. Mr. Lincoln had not yet given out his course of policy, and if he had, and that policy proved objectionable to the Southern leaders, all that they had to do was to remedy their wrong either real or imaginary in a constitutional and legal manner. But they chose to rebel and commit their traitorous, treasonable rebellions, overt acts to destroy the government.

The results in the main are now matters of history, and all the peculiar facts with regard to horrors, suffering, devastation. The heroism, and patriotism of our soldiers are from day to day being brought to light, and will also soon become matters of history. To do our share in placing facts before the world, and aid in making up the history is to give the history of the captivity of a fellow soldier, his sufferings and experience in the South during nineteen months imprisonment. The man who left a good situation to shoulder a musket as a private. A sacrifice that was as great to him personally as that of any general connected with history of this war.

James S. Anderson was born on a farm in Genesee County, N. Y. At the age of 15 years he was to be found in Michigan, some way connected with the laying the track of the Michigan Central Railroad. When the track was laid he took the position of fireman on the Engine. Went to Chicago in 1850, and followed one sort or another of railroading two years, and then came to Milwaukee, Wisconsin; where he pursued the business of railroading, mainly on the Milwaukee and Mississippi Railroad, until the spring of the year 1856, when he received the appointment of Locomotive Engineer, on the La Crosse and Milwaukee Railroad, where he remained until he joined the army. He joined the 24th Regiment Wisconsin Volunteers, Co. F., August 21st, 1862, as a private, and was mustered in at the same time.

Now what inducement could there be, excepting pure patriotism to induce a young man like Mr. Anderson to leave his position and go into the army at $13, per month? He was receiving a good salary and stood in an excellent place in the esteem of the company and others for promotion. There was no draft to fear, there was no inducement but to save the country.

Mr. Anderson is a stout built, over medium sized man, with great power of endurance displayed in every move he makes. Whether on business or fun, he gives his whole attention to it. He is popular with his employers because he never neglects his duty or comes in with excuses. He is jovial and full of fun on a frolic, but place him on duty and he has nothing to do with anything that is not connected with his business.

Anderson's muscle or strength is proverbial among those who know him. His cordiality seems to be equal to his strength. At one time on being introduced to a stranger, a railroad man like himself, they shook hands. Anderson, being perhaps, in a cordial mood, and perhaps, taking a fancy to his new made acquaintance, shook hands with an honest, well meant, and true cordiality, saying: "I have heard of you, glad to make your acquaintance. Stranger answered: "Oh! I am happy to make your acquaintance, but for pity's sake don't squeeze my hand so hard." His great muscular strength arises undoubtedly, from his early and continued training in muscular pursuits, such as handling railroad iron, locomotives, etc., and may account in a measure for his living through his hard campaign as a prisoner. Anderson is unyielding, inflexible, and never forsook a friend or forgot a favor.

CHAPTER II.

THE DAYS WHEN WE WENT GYPSYING.

On going into camp at Camp Sigel, Milwaukee, nearly every soldier enjoyed the change. In camping out there, the regiment seemed to be following the fashion of the Gypsies. Discipline, to be sure was introduced under our vigilant Colonel, as soon as possible, but that could not be done in an hour, a day, or in a week. Many a fine fellow who thought, at Camp Sigel, that soldiering was one of the finest things in the world, soon after the celebrated campaign, under Gen. Buell, in pursuit of Bragg, found that whether soldiering had many attractions or not, depended very much upon what kind of a General was in command. Anderson went through that campaign and participated in the Perryville or Chaplain Hills battle, went with the army to Crab Orchard, where Gen. Buell seemed to be placed in nearly the same position as that of the King of France, who

"With seventy thousand men,
Marched up the hill and then marched back again."

Gen. Buell had 60,000 men when he started in pursuit of Bragg, from Louisville, Kentucky, and when he started back on his track more than 10,000 were in hospital or their graves, with the lasting disgrace of letting what might be called a mere squad, hold our army in check at Perryville, while the rebels carted off the plunder which they had been several months in collecting together.

Anderson being intelligent and posted upon what was going

on, denounced with an almost indiscreet fury, the whole transaction; but he seems determined to always speak his mind. A great many of the officers and men did the same thing, but no one was court martialed or punished, because, probably, Gen. Buell had become aware of what was soon to be his own fate. When the army reached Nashville, Buell was removed and Gen. Rosencrans took command, and by him was fought the great battle of Stone River.

Mr. Anderson was at his post in front and escaped withotu a wound. It may as well be remarked here that the 24th Regiment was a portion of the right wing, under command of Gen. Johnson, and that the brigade was under the command of Gen. Sill; and also, that the 24th Regiment did not leave the field until three acting brigade commanders were dead on the field, namely, Generals Sill, Roberts and Schafer. Nor did they retire until Johnson's right had been completely turned with the loss of a great number of men, and 27 cannon and the enemy commenced firing in the rear, which they gained through Gen. Johnson's culpable negligence. This occurred on Wednesday, the 31st of December, but on the Friday following, by a stragetic move, Gen. Rosencrans, driven almost to the last extremity, drew the enemy into a snare and gained his victory.

The 24th Regiment remained in or near Murfreesboro until the 24th of June, 1863, and then started on the Tullahoma Campaign. Their business at Murfreesboro was only fortifying, picketing and foraging. In this march the Union army reached Cowan, sixty or sixty-five miles, on the 3d day of July. The object was to give the rebel Gen. Bragg battle. In the cautious movements in manoeuvering, the army moved slowly and was out thirteen days, marching knee deep through mud and water. After all this Bragg was found to have retreated and of course no battle was fought.

The rains had swollen the streams to an unusual degree, but they must be crossed *nolens volens*. Elk river in particular, seemed to be on the "rampage." Cables were placed across the stream to aid the soldier's to wade, nearly neck deep, across the seething waters. Nor was this all, a strong cavalry force was placed below the ford to rescue those who met with any mishap.

When it came the turn for Gen. Lytle's Brigade to cross, the General rode up to the men and said: "This crossing by the cable is too slow, will you take a regular march right through just to show them that some things can be done as well as others."

It so happened that Anderson was in the vanguard, and for the first time in his life hesitated. The water seemed to deep and rapid. He looked around among his companions and seeing Moffatt, a taller man than himself, said: "Moffatt, you are the taller, suppose you try the depth of water first, I'll follow." "Agreed," said Moffatt, and he plunged in without any ceremony. But missing his step in jumping, he went down out of sight. Being a good swimmer and, perhaps, a little irritated at his misadventure, he called out: "Come on boys, I found the bottom and so can you if you try." The men at once plunged in and crossed the river without the loss of a man.

From Cowan the command marched to Bridgeport and was immediately put on picket duty, watching the rebels, who were under the command of Gen. Bragg, and were posted on a large island near the opposite shore of the river. The bridge, nearly a half mile long had already been partially destroyed by the retreating rebels.

The Union batteries were placed in position, those of Gen. Lytle commanding the bridge and its approaches, with Capt. Schutemeister in command.

On the 15th of August, about 11 o'clock in the evening, the vigilant Captain rushed up to Gen. Lytle's head-quarters and cried out at the top of his stentorian voice: "Sheneral Lytle, Sheneral Lytle! de pridge is on fire, shall I open my batteries."

The General, in his usual cool manner, replied: "Yes, I guess you had better give them a few shots, just to show them that we are around."

The shots were given by the valient Captain but it was of no use, the enemy had evacuated, and it would probably have taken a gun of fifteen miles range to reach their rear guard.

Chapter III.

THE CHICAMAUGA CAMPAIGN.

ANDERSONS PARTICIPATION—HIS CAPTURE, ESCAPE AND RE-CAPTURE.

The corps, under the command of Gen. McCook, started from Bridgeport on the Chicamauga Campaign on the 2d day of September, 1863. Gen. Lytle's Brigade was a portion of that command.

At this time Anderson was a member of the non-commissioned staff of Gen. Lytle, which position he held up to the time of his capture. Gen. McCook's Corps was intended and dispatched as a feeler or flanker. His first move was to some undefined point in a direction South of West of Bridgeport, and some sixty miles distant. The corps then moved in a south-easterly direction, and crossed Lookout Mountain for the first time, and reached Alpine, only twenty-four miles from Rome, on Saturday, the 12th. After remaining there about twenty-four hours, a retrogade movement was ordered. Pursuing a northerly course, the command for the second time ascended Lookout Mountain and camped on the western slope for one day, and then pursued a mountain road in a northeastterly direction. In all this movement, so far into the enemy's country, it so happened that no resisting army was found and consequently there was no fight.

The command reached the Chicamauga battle field, late in the night of Saturday the 20th. There had been pretty heavy fighting that day, and the right wing, where Gen. Lytle immediately after his arrival took position, was found in a somewhat disorganized and confused condition. No further battle was considered as probable, for the reason that the preceeding day's work had been very exhausting to both sides and that a recuperation by repose would be necessary. Furthermore it was the Sabbath, a day of rest.

The killed and wounded had only been partially taken care of, but about 9 A. M., the Rebels opened fire and the bloody contest was at once inaugurated, the main feature of which have become familiar to all, and as the writers purpose or inclination do not lead him to compile this bloody page in history, it is omitted, and we pass on to the time of Anderson's capture, this took place about noon on the same day.

As before remarked the right wing was found in some confusion, this increased as the battle proceed, and Anderson and others found themselves completely enveloped by the emeny who were driving the Union forces—they were made prisoners. Directly afterwards an Illinois Regiment made a furious attack on that portion of the rebel lines in which Anderson was held and drove the enemy back. It was at this time that Anderson gave the guard the slip, and concealed himself. This was only an escape from the guard. The enemy fleeing and the Union forces pursuing, passed him in his hiding place. The contest was raging with such violence just then, that it was very difficult to tell the position of friend or foe. A great many of the rebels wore the U. S. blue uniform, which made the case more embarrassing. The first thing to be thought of as soon as prudence would allow, was to find the Union lines, and get into them if possible. This was a very difficult piece of business for several reasons. The woods were dense and the under brush formed a complete thicket. The position of no portion of either army was known to Anderson, to add to the trouble he come on the ground in the dark of the night, and when the conflict commenced in the morning he had not found his bearings. On looking around he found a few of his comrades in the same position as himself. All at their wits ends to know what to do or which way to move. After a careful reconnoitering of the position, and a full consultation as to what was to be done, they started in the direction decided upon. They had not gone far before they came upon private Grunanger one of their comrades of the 24th, who was wounded in the knee. He was as anxious to get his regiment as they were, but could give them no information as to the position of either friend or foe. His wound was so severe that he could not move a step. Anderson and his friends took him up and carried him a half mile, when it became apparent to all parties concerned that it was simply a waste of stregth and time, they laid him down by a tree, built him a fire and left him some water, they also told him that if they were in the Union lines, and if it proved in the line of possibilities they would send or bring him such relief as his case demanded. They however soon found that they were powerless to help either their wounded comrade or themselves. They were like a ship at sea, without pilot or compass. In the twilight of the evening in wandering about they came to a road and met soldiers in blue carrying wounded men from the field. Anderson at once suggested that they looked like rebels in the disguise of the U. S. uniform. The sudden meeting was so unexpected to both parties, each seemed a little confused. No one seemed inclined to speak the first word. After a short pause one of the men engaged in carrying the wounded broke silence by enquiring of Anderson in a tone and manner not easily misunderstood as follows; "I say stranger kin you tell me where Day's Hospital is?" Days' Hospital was an exclusive rebel institution. That question decided at once that they were rebels, and as they were armed, and our men were not, and furthermore outnumbering our little band two to one. Anderson and his party answered just as much as they chose and left at once for the woods and bushes. Before they got out of the hearing of the conversation of their new made acquaintances, they had the pleasure of hearing one of them remark. "Why they look like Yanks."

CHAPTER IV.

JAMES S. ANDERSON FINALLY CAPTURED.

> "Society, friendship and love,
> Divinity bestowed upon man,
> Oh! had I the wings of a dove,
> How soon would I taste you again.
>
> My sorrows then might I assuage,
> In the ways of religion and truth,
> Might lean from the wisdom of age,
> And be cheered by the sallies of youth."

After escaping as related in the preceeding chapter, it being, after getting a sufficient distance from the rebels, quite dark, the little party bivouacked without fire or any other convenience until daylight appeared. With daylight the party started again on its tramp at random "the usual way," and they "met by chance," what! a brigade of Rebel Cavalry, who rode furiously toward them, and the leader in a loud voice, cried out, "You d——n Yankee, surrender." The summons had to be obeyed of course.

Here begins the troubles, experience and hardships of Anderson. The first thing he had to encounter at the hands of the chivalry, in the way of insult, followed his capture at once.

One of the chivalry, armed with a revolver rode up to him and demanded, "have you got any jack-knife;" the answer was "yes." "Let me see it," demanded chivalry. Chivalry looked at it, seemed to admire it, wanted it, offered $10 in confederate money, but did not make a trade. The only wonder is that he did not put it into his pocket, but he did not, he handed it back.

This specimen of mankind, who seemed to think he was emulating Don Quixote or some other great lord, was a lad of sixteen, or thereabouts, with a coon-skin cap on his head, and a uniform on his body to match. A vulgar little wretch who would, in any well regulated city in the United States, be sent to the Reform School, or some worse place.

The Colonel commanding, had a negro on his horse behind him which he had captured from our side, and was *carrying him about in that way for sale.* Oh! my gracious! What a fall was there, my countrymen. A Confederate Colonel on duty, lugging a nigger about, on horseback, on the same horse with himself, and while on duty in command of a brigade. Comment is unnecessary.

It was the pleasure of the rebel authorities to send the prisoners to Ringgold, a distance by the nearest route, of thirteen miles. But for some reason they were marched through heat and dust in the day time and camped under guard, at night time in the proverbial cold of this region, without shelter or provisions. But perhaps, the prisoners sufferings were somewhat mitigated by the fact that they passed through Gen. Breckenridge's camp and saw them issuing two day's rations to the soldiers of his invincible army.

It may be well to remark here that Gen. Breckenridge had been Vice President of the United States. The position next in importance to the destines of mankind that could be confered on mortal man. In an evil he forgot his duty to his country to his God, and the lasting interest of mankind and joined the rebellion with avowed purpose of destroying the best Government that the sun ever shone upon so far as history can enlighten us on that point, and also the one which conferred upon him those stupendous honors and responsibilities. What was Gen. Breckenridge doing when our troops were passing their lines. He was issuing two days rations to his men, all consisting of two pieces of sugar cane each being about one foot long. The soldiers were in general ragged, barefooted and dirty. Gen. Breckenridge would have been ashamed to march this awkward unwashed squad through any respectable city or town in christendom. Poor Breckenridge your case cannot but call to recollection the immortal lines of Moore.

> "The harps that once thro Taras Walls,
> The Saul of music Shed,
> Now hangs as mute on Taras Wall
> As if that Soul were flew
>
> So sleeps the pride of former days,
> So glory's thrill is oer
> And hearts that once beat high with pain.
> Now feel that throb no more.

You are now a fugitive in a strange land, probably never to return to that glorious country which you so ingloriously deserted, certainly never to indulge in those gay and festive scenes which in former times gave you so much delight.

On Tuesday, the 22d of March, the prisoners were marched to Tunnel Hill, there being about 3,000 prisoners in all, in the line of march. Where they were going, no one knew. At this point, Col. West, of the 24th Wisconsin, was met, he was also a prisoner.

Here an aggravating circumstance occurred. Orders had been given to issue two day's rations to each prisoner. The rations were piled up in plain sight of the prisoners but before they were distributed, marching orders were given, and away the prisoners marched with an "aching void," and no ration to supply the deficiency.

This was not the end of the catastrophe. In going out of the prison pen, in passing the gate the rubber blankets and canteens were, by orders from head-quarters, taken from each prisoner as he passed the guard. Anderson's rubber was wrapped tightly in his woolen blanket and escaped. Finding that his canteen was in very great danger of seizure he took it from his person, placed it upon the ground and a single well directed stamp with his foot, placed the canteen beyond the hope of usefulness. When he got out of the reach of observation he gave his rubber blanket to Col. West, because it was not customary to take such things from officers.

When the prisoners were finally formed into line, the rebels evidently wanted to impress the Yankees at parting with an exagerated idea of their power, brought out the Georgia Militia, armed with great wooden swords. The prisoners could not help notwithstanding their exhausted condition, feeling slightly mirthful, and by a few well directed questions dispersed, in a few minutes, of this specimen of chivalry.

On Thursday, the 22d day of September, the prisoners were marched to Dalton and went into camp and drew rations—a pint of flour, with nothing to cook it in, mixed it with water and put it into the ashes to cook. When it was about half done orders came to fall in and of course the prisoners cake was dough.

The object of making the men fall in was simply to march them through the town for exhibition. There was a large and intelligent audience on hand of both sexes. They called out as the prisoners passed—"you vandals," "you uns can't never subjugate weones, &c., &c. After the exhibition was over, the prisoners were marched back to camp again.

The next morning they were taken to Atlanta about 100 miles distant, when they arrived at about 4 P. M., Wednesday, Sept. 23d, and were marched by a long route through the City. The gaping crowd stared at them—but they had the good fortune to get good camping ground. This was however accidental. It so happened that the rebels had to quarter a large number of their own deserters in the town at the same time. They had already got possession of the old vermin besieged quarters, and it was dangerous to undertake to change matters under the circumstances, and thus it happened that our boys got their excellent quarters.

The next day a regular detail of men was sent from the head quarters of the rebels to take from the prisoners their woolen blankets and jack-knives, they were marched through a narrow gate, and each man halted and relieved of his blanket at once, and then the hands of one of those authorized agents were thrust into the pockets of the victims in search of jack knives and other plunder. Col. West of the 24th Wisconsin witnessing the outrage vehemently remonstrated—a dirty looking confederate Captain, whose wearing apparel seemed to have been a stranger to change for many months, and whose face and hands indicated a "total abstinance" from water several weeks, called out "you needn't talk, they serve you right, you uns robbed me at Camp Chase, you took the shirt off my back." Anderson was standing near, and promptly answered, "well then they gave you a clean one in the place of it." This raised such a shout among both rebels and union men that the dirty Captain left.— The next night was very cold and the men suffered greatly. In the morning at day light the prisoners drew five days rations and started for the cars, bound to Richmond. At that time the prisoners numbered about 4000, but only about 2000 went by this train. Large number of people were on the ground to see the Northern vandals on their arrival at the depot, and as they had to wait two or three hours at the depot, their curiosity had that length of time for gratification.

While these precious secession specimens were gratifying their curiosity, they did not themselves escape observation, and it was found that in the sin of omission they were entitled to a page in history. Whether it was also a sin of commission divines must decide.

Two trains of cars with wounded confederate soldiers came to the depot and halted long enough to receive humane attention at least. There was no more attention paid to them by the gaping rebel crowd than as though they were so many cattle. No provision was offered, no attention paid to their appeals for water. None of the men who had pledged with these soldiers their lives, their fortunes, and their sacred honor to sustain the rebellion went to their relief. This is a case which might justify Oliver Goldsmiths expressed idea of friendship, when he says.

> And what is friendship but a name,
> A charm that lulls to sleep:
> A shade that follows wealth and fame.
> And leaves the wretch to weep.

CHAPTER V.

ON THE WAY TO RICHMOND AND BELLE ISLE.

A PLEASANT CAMPING GROUND—INCIDENTS—AN ENCOUNTER—A FIGHT.

From Dalton after considerable delay the prisoners proceeded in freight cars towards Richmond, the Capital of the Confederacy. They had by some means learned their destination, the horrors of Libby prison of course was presented to their views with a strong suspicion that they were to be the recipients of "Southern hospitality" in that celebrated institution.

In pursuing their journey reached Augusta, about 170 miles from Dalton, at about 1 o'clock A. M., of the next day. At Augusta, the prisoners were placed in the Baptist Church yard, a beautiful piece of ground, tastefully laid out and ornamented and shaded by the Magnolia and other ornamental trees, some hopes was indulged by a few of the enthusiastic that this might be the place of their future abode until exchanged. Early in the morning however the illusion was dispelled by the order to fall in, and at 8 o'clock Saturday the 26th found the unfortunates on their winding way, and the next day at noon they found themselves in Columbia. At every place of importance along the line at which the trains stopped large numbers of people were assembled to take a long lasting look or stare at the dreaded "Yanks."

After a few hours stay at Columbia, the prisoners were taken by railroad to Chester, about 40 miles distant. A large number of people came out to see the Yanks, and among them a very great many nabobs. Charleston at that time was being bombarded, and the wealthy non-combattants congregated at this point by some kind of instinct, perhaps, simply for the reason, "that birds of a feather flock together."

The next place reached was Charlotte, N. C., which place was reached about two o'clock in the morning, where the prisoners were allowed the privilege of remaining until day light, and then they proceeded to Salisbury, about 40 or 50 miles This place contains one of the Regular Military prisons. From Salisbury they proceeded to Greensboro where a slight incident occured The people as usual along the route turned out to see what kind of a creature a "Yank" really appeared like. They had evidently been led to believe in one or two things that they were frightful monsters, dangerous to approach without the precaution of chaining them or placing them in secure cages or else they were mean cowardly vandals. Of course in a small place there must of necessity be two parties. One believed in the idea that the Yanks were cowards and the other that they were not. In one thing they were all agreed, and that was that the Yanks were placed in a condition in which it would not be dangerous to go and see them. They therefore went with the same feelings and emotions that people experience in going to a menagarie. After getting on the ground and seeing that the prisoners were simply men, and waiting a short time for their nerves to get quieted, the valorous gentlemen who had expressed the popular opinion that the "Yank" were cowards, began to be abusive, calling the prisoners "Yanks," "vandals," cowards &c., interlarding their expressions with indecent slang and profanity. One of them who seemed to be a leader, became so furious in his denunciations that he soon attracted general attention Perceiving that he was the observed of all observers he became more abusive and violent, and finally talked himself into courage enough to approach the cars still uttering his denunciations against the Government and the Northern people. One of the prisoners in the cars felt so outraged at the language used by this specimen of chivalry that he jumped from the car, passed the guard in a twinking, and gave the bragadocia a sound thrashing in less than two minutes, and then quietly returned to his place in the car.

The guard finding that things might grow serious, went to work and cleared the ground of all the brawlers and gazers. The prisoners route from Greensboro, was through Raleigh and Weldon, arriving at Petersburg, September 30th, and were marched through the town in the dark in order to prevent the prisoners seeing or making any observations with regard to the rebel fortifications. After getting out of town, they were placed on the cars and went to Richmond, 22 miles, and the same day marched to Belle Island. Belle Island, by its name, might seem to be a very pleasant place, and under some circumstances, in times gone by, was, but the boys in Blue did not find it so ; that is, the Western ones did not. They had no shelter. Their clothes were very thin and scanty, and the weather was remarkably and severely cold. The prisoners had to walk all night to keep from freezing. To add to the misery, the rations served out were scanty and unwholesome. They consisted of one quarter loaf of very poor bread, one ounce of what was called beef, but which had a very small title to the name, a few buggy, goober peas, and all this ready cooked in rebel style. And yet the men were reduced to such an extremity, that they awaited with impatience and anxiety their arrival and distribution. They were cooked at a distance from the camp, and were brought there by a steamer.

The vile trash which was to supply the "aching void" of an empty Stomach, was so longed for by the famished men, that no vessel ever approached shore that was more cordially welcomed than this conveyer of garbage was every morning by the half famished prisoners. In the early part of December the cold became intense, and many prisoners froze to death. How many, cannot be ascertained at present—but it is certain, that in one night, six died by freezing.

RETURN TO RICHMOND.

PRISON LIFE THERE UNDER JEFF. DAVIS' PERSONAL OBSERVATION EVERY DAY. HE COULD NOT HELP KNOWING THE CONDITION OF THINGS OCCURRING EVERY DAY "RIGHT UNDER HIS NOSE" IN HIS PRETENDED ESTABLISHED CAPITOL.

On the fifth of March the prisoners were or ordered to fall in. Such as could do so obeyed the order, and were marched to Richmond, passing over Long bridge, which is from one quarter to one half mile long. The line of march gave the men a chance to see Castle Thunder to their left. Libby prison which was on the right hand, and Pemberton prison, where they turned the corner and went into what is called Smith's building, formerly used as a tobacco warehouse. They were placed in the third story.

There a man known by the name of little Ross or Jack of Clubs came up to call the roll. If any of the men were tardy about falling in he would scold in a loud voice, and kick and cuff them, pretty soon he became so odious that the prisoners would call out *en masse* on his making his appearance "Jack of Clubs," "Jack of Clubs," this at first made him still more furious, but in the end had the effect to make him a little more decent in his deportment.

If any prisoner made his appearance at the window, a sentry would call out, "Tuck your head in thar," and at the same time blaze away with his musket without any regard as to whom he would hit.

A little incident occured here which may be worthy of mention—Frederick Reynor of Gen. Sheridan's Staff made his escape. By some means or other he got into his possession an artillery officers suit of uniform, and after having put it on with due care and exactness, was prepared to emerge. As usual the prisoners were crowded as near the guard as possible. Reynor marched down the stairs in a pompous manner, and demanded of the guards, why they did not make d——m——d Yanks stand back, and remarked that there was "hardly room for a gentleman to pass in and out." The guards stood in awe of this august personage, and he marched by them. The last that was seen of him he was eating one loaf of bread and carrying another under his arm. A convenient baker shop furnished him these much needed supplies, and he deliberately marched out of the rebel lines, and was never recaptured.

The little pompous man Ross was in the habit when coming to call the roll of bringing with him his favorite dog. The prisoners caught him one day, and after the redoubtable little man had left—cooked and ate [him. This may in some way show to what an extremity of hungry men were driven to in the capitol of the confederacy.

The rations at this place came cooked, but were cold before reaching the prison. The man in charge scooped out with his hands what he thought proper ration for each prisoner. For a a while the prisoners warmed their cold lunch by gas, but an order came from head-quarters forbidding the use of gas in that way.

There were several changes in prisons with all the events and incidents connected with the various moves while the prisoners were confined in Richmond.

But as we are in somewhat of a hurry to reach the main point of interest, Andersonville, only one other fact will be related, of Capt. Turner, Provost Marshall of Richmond. He came to the prisoners and said he had orders to receive all the money and proceeded to take the same, putting the names of the men and the amounts in a seeming official book, promising to return the same at a proper time. In this way he got a very large amount of money, but pay day has never come. In fact it might be remarked that the jingle of money in an empty pocket returns no "sound." The experience of the prisoners at Richmond was not much varied excepting they were placed first in one prisons and then another until their final departure for Andersonville.

Departure from Richmond. Arrival at Andersonville Meeting and Greeting of Capt Wirz.

The 16th of May found Anderson leaving No. 4 prison for Andersonville, passing through Greensboro, Charlotte, Augusta and Allen, and arriving at Andersonville on the 21st of May, at 5 P. M., when Capt. Henry Wirz was met for the first time, who exclaimed in triumph " now I show you tam Yanks! I'm an officer of de grand army. " Fall into line dere." The soldiers being somewhat tired were slow in their movements. Wirz exclaimed, " I had my preakfast, I had my tinner, I don't care one tam. You gets no supper 'till you opeys my orders." The result was that the men got no supper. Henry Wirz is a tall cadavarous Swiss, about six feet high, stooping shoulders, who bent nearly double in riding his grey mare, with a narrow forehead, eyes close together, whiskers straggling, features sharp.

He would draw his revolvers quite frequently, always accompanying the act with some threat. He invariably, when irritated, showed his teeth, which were neither clean or regular; but as Captain Wirz is on trial and his case and charges in indictment are now transpiring, we will place him in the position that the newspaper reports place him, reserving the right to make such future comments as may seem proper. The newspapers give him the following description, viz: The appearance of Henry Wirz at the commencement of his trial before the military commission in Washington is thus described:

"He is a slenderly built man, about forty-five or fifty years of age, with dark hair and whiskers streaked with grey. He was dressed in a black suit, and a white shirt. On the way from the Old Capitol Prison to the Court Room he wore an old fashioned silk hat. During the reading of the charges, he sat between his counsel, with whom he conversed frequently. He sat with his legs crossed and his hand to his face and manifested at times considerable nervousness."

The charges and specifications are given below.

TRIAL OF WIRZ.

CHARGES OFFICIALLY.

WASHINGTON, August 21, 1865.

The special military commission convened at the Court of Claims' room, Major-General Wallace presiding, and Colonel Chipman Judge Advocate. At half-past one o'clock Captain Wirz, the prisoner to be tried, was brought into the room, guarded on each side by a soldier. The prisoner was requested to rise, when Colonel Chipman said: "Captain Wirz, you are to be tried by this military commission. Have you any personal objection to any of its members?" Judge Hughes, of the counsel, said he proposed to make no objection of a personal character. They would, however, at a subsequent stage of the proceedings, ask to be heard on the plea of a general jurisdiction, especially objecting to the mode of constituting the court; but if the prisoner was to be tried by a military commission, he would as soon be tried by this one as any other. The members of the commission were then sworn. The Judge Advocate informed the prisoner that he was arraigned for trial under the name of Henry Wirz. Was that the name? The prisoner answered that it was. Judge Hughes desired to say that the charges and specifications were not delivered to the prisoner until yesterday afternoon, and were not seen by his counsel this morning; therefore they had not sufficient time to examine them. Colonel Chipman said that the counsel could ask for delay after arraignment, and then proceeded to read the charges and specifications against Henry Wirz, as follows:

CHARGE FIRST.—Maliciously, willfully and traitorously, and in aid of the then existing armed rebellion against the United States of America, of, on, or before the first day of March, A. D. 1864, and on divers other days between that day and the tenth day of April, 1865, combining, confederating and conspiring, together with Robert E. Lee, James A. Seddon, John H. Winder, Lucius D. Northrup, Richard B. Winder, Joseph White, W. S. Winder, R. R. Stevenson, Moore, and others unknown, to injure the health and destroy the lives of soldiers in the military service of the United States, then held and being prisoners of war within the lines of the so-called confederate states, in the military prisons thereof, to the end that the armies of the United States might be weakened and impaired, in violation of the laws and customs of war.

SPECIFCATION.—In this that the said Henry Wirz did combine, confederates and and conspired with them, the said Robert E. Lee, Joseph A. Seddon, John H. Winder, Lucius H. Northrup, R. B. Winder, Joseph White, W. S. Winder, R. R.

Stevenson, more and others whose names are unknown, citizens of the United States, aforesaid, and who were then engaged in armed rebellion against the United States, malaciously, traitorously, and in violation of the laws of war, to impair and injure the health, and to destroy their lives by subjecting them to torture and great suffering by confining in unhealthy and unwholesome quarters, by exposing to the inclemency of the weather and to the dews and the burning sun, of summer by compelling the use of impure water and by furnishing insufficient and unwholesome food, of large numbers of federal soldiers in the military service of the U. S. of America, held prisoners of war at Andersonville, in the state of Georgia, within the lines of the so called confederate states, on or before the first day of March, A. D. 1864, and at divers times between that day and the 10th day of April, A. D. 1865, to the end that the armies of the U. S. might be weakened and impaired, and the insurgents engaged in armed rebellion against the U. S., might be aided and comforted and helped, said Henry Wirz, and officer in the so called confederate states, being then and there commandant of a military prison at Andersonville, in the state of Georgia, located by authority of the so called confederate states, for the confinement of prisoners of war, and as such commandant, fully clothed with authority, and in duty bound to treat, care and provide for such prisoners held as aforesaid as were or might be placed in his custody according to the laws of war, did in furtherance of such combination, confederation and conspiracy and entered thereinto by them—the said Robert E. Lee, Jas. A. Seddon, John H. Winder, Lucius H. Northrup, Richard B. Winder, Jas. White, W. S. Winder, R. R. Stevenson, Moore, and others whose names are unknown, maliciously wickedly, and traitorously confined a large number of such prisoners of war soldiers in the military service of the United States to the amount of 30,000 men in unhealthy and unwholsome quarters, and in a close and small area of ground wholly inadequate to their wants and destructive to their health, which he well knew and intended, and while there so confined during the time aforesaid, did in furtherance of his evil design and in aid of the said conspiracy wilfully and maliciously neglected to furnish tents, barracks or other shelter for their protection from the inclemency of winter, and dews and burning sun of summer ; and with such intent did take and cause to be taken from them their clothing, blankets, camp equipage and other property of which they were possessed at the time of being placed in his custody; and with like malice and evil intent did refuse to furnish or cause to be furnished food, either of a quality or quantity sufficient to preserve health and sustain life, and did refuse and neglect to furnish wood sufficient for cooking in summer and to keep the said prisoners warm in the winter ; and did compel the said prisoners to subsist upon unwholesome water, reeking with the filth of garbage of the prison and prison yard, and the offial and drainage of the back house of said prison, whereby the prisoners became greatly reduced in their bodily strength and emaciated and injured in their bodily health, their minds impaired and their intellects broken, and many of them to-wit : Ten thousand whose names are unknown sickened and died by reason thereof, which he, said Henry Wirz, then and there well knew and intended, and so knowing, and evily intending, did refuse and neglect to provide proper lodging, food or nourishment for the sick, and necessary medicine and medical attendance for the restoration of their health, and did knowingly, maliciously and wilfully, in furtherance of his evil designs, permit them to languish and die from want of care and proper treatment.

And the said Henry Wirz, still pursuing his evil purposes, did permit to remain in the said prison, among the emaciated, sick and languishing living, the bodies of the dead until they became corrupt and loathsome, and filled the air with fetid and noxious exhalations, and thereby greatly increased the unwholesomeness of the prison, inasmuch that great numbers of the said prisoners, to wit, to the number of ten thousand, whose names are unknown, sickened and died by reason thereof.

And the said Henry Wirz, still pursuing his wicked and cruel purpose, wholly disregarding the usages and rules of civilized warfare, did, at the time and place aforesaid, maliciously and wilfully subject the prisoner aforesaid to cruel, unusual and infamous punishment, upon slight, trivial and fictitious pretences, by fastening large balls of iron to their feet, and binding large numbers of the prisonors closely together with large chains around their necks and feet, so that they walked with the greatest difficulty, and being so confined were subjected to the burning rays of the sun, and often without any food or drink for hours and every day, from which said cruel treatment large numbers, to wit: the numbes of one hundred, whose names are unknown, sickened, fainted, and died.

And, he, the said Wirz did further cruelly treat and injure said prisoners, by maliciously confining them within an instrument of torture called the stocks, thus depriving them of the use of their limbs, and forcing them to lie still and stand for many hours without the power of changing position, and being without food or drink, in consequence of which many, to wit: the number of thirty whose names are unknown, sickened and died.

And he, the said Wirz, still wickedly pursuing his evil purposes, did establish and cause to be designated within the prison enclosure containing said prisoners, a dead line, being a line around the inner face of the stockade or wall enclosing said prison, and about twenty feet distant from and within said stockade, and having so established said dead line, which was in many places an imaginary line and in many other places marked by insecure and shifting strips of boards nailed upon the tops of small and insecure stakes or posts, he, the said Wirz instructed the prison guards stationed around the said stockade, to fire upon and kill any of the prisoners aforesaid who might touch, fall upon, pass over or under, or across the said dead line, pursuant to which said orders maliciously and needlessly given by said Wirz, the said prison guard did fire upon and kill a large number of said prisoners, to wit: the number of about three hundred.

And the said Wirz, still pursuing his evil purpose, did keep and use ferocious and blood-thirsty beasts, dangerous to human life, called bloodhounds, to hunt down prisoners of war, aforesaid, who made their escape from his custody, and did then and there wilfully and maliciously suffer, excite and encourage the said beasts to seize, tear, mangle and maim the bodies and limbs of said fugitive prisoners of war, which the said beasts incited as aforesaid, then and there did, whereby a large number of said prisoners of war, who, during the time aforesaid, made their escape and were recaptured, and were by said beasts then and there cruelly and inhumanly injured, inasmuch that many of said prisoners, to wit: the number of about fifty died.

And the said Wirz still pursuing his wicked purpose, and still aiding in carrying out said conspiracy, did use and cause to be used for the pretended purpose of vaccination, vaccine matter which same impure and poisonous matter was then and there, by the direction and order of said Wirz, maliciously, cruelly and wickedly deposited in the arms of many of said prisoners, by reason of which large numbers of them, to-wit: one hundred lost their arms, and many of them, to-wit: about the number of two hundred were so injured that they soon thereafter died, all of which the said Henry Wirz well knew and maliciously intended, and in aid of the then existing rebellion against the United States, with a view to assist in weakening and impairing the armies of the United States, and in furtherance of the said conspiracy, and with the full knowledge, consent and connivance of his conspirators aforesaid, the said Wirz, then and there, did—

CHARGE 2.—Murder in violation of the laws and customs of war.

SPECIFICATION 1.—In this the said H. Wirz, an officer in the rebel service of the so-called confederate states, at Andersonville, in the State of Georgia, on or about the 8th day of July, A. D. 1864, then and there being commandant of a prison there located by the authority of said so-called confederate states for the confinement of prisoners of war taken and held as such from the armies of the United States, while acting as said commandant, feloniously, willfully, and of his malice aforethought, did make an assault, and he, the said Wirz, with a revolver, then and there loaded and charged with gun-powder and bullets, which said pistol the said Wirz, in his hand then and there, had and held to, against and upon a soldier belonging to the army of the United States, in his, the said Henry Wirz's custody as a prisoner of war, whose name is unknown, then and there feloniously, and of his malice aforethought, did shoot and discharge, inflicting upon the body of the soldier aforesaid a mortal wound with the pistol aforesaid, in consequence of which said mortal wound, murderously inflicted by said Wirz, the said soldier thereafter died.

SPECIFICATION 2.—In this that said Henry Wirz, an officer in the military service of the so called Confederate States of America, at Andersonville, in the State of Georgia, on or about the 20th day of September, A. D. 1865, then and there being commandant of a prison there located by authority of the so called Confederate States, for the confinement of prisoners of war taken, and held as such, from the armies of the United States, while acting as said commandant, feloniously, wilfully and of his malice aforethought, did jump upon, stamp, kick, bruise, and otherwise injure with the heels of his boots a soldier belonging to the army of the United States in his, the said Wirz custody as a prisoner of war, whose name is unknown and of which said soldier soon thereafter died.

SPECIFICATION 3—In this that said Wirz, an officer in the military service of the so-called confederate states at Andersonville, in the State of Georgia, on or about the 13th day of June, A. D. 1864, then and there being commandant of a prison there located by authority of said so-called confederates for the confinement of prisoners of war, taken and held as such from the armies of the United States of America while acting as commandant, feloniously and of his malice aforethought, did make an assault, and he, the said Wirz, with a certain pistol, called revolver, then and there loaded and charged with gunpowder and bullets, which said pistol the said Henry Wirz in hand then and there held against and upon a soldier belonging to the army, a prisoner of war, whose name is unknown, then and there feloniously, and of his malice aforethought, did shoot and discharge, inflicting upon the body of the soldier aforesaid, a mortal wound with the pistol aforesaid, in consequence of which said mortal wound, murderously inflicted by the said Wirz, the said soldier thereafter died.

The amended charges and action of the Military commission and counsel for defendant are as follows :

THE WIRZ TRIAL.

WASHINGTON, Aug. 23, 1865.

The Wirz commission met this morning. Colonel Chipman read an order from the war department dated yesterday, dissolving the former commission but appointing another, consisting of the same members who were again sworn in to-day, and Captain Wirz again arraigned. when the charges and specifications were read. They are in the main, substantially the same as those heretofore presented. The alterations include the striking out of the names of Robert E. Lee, James A. Seddon and Lucius D. Northrop, as some of those with whom the prisoner is is accused of combining and conspiring to impair and injure the health and to destroy the lives, by subjecting to torture and great suffering, of large numbers of federal prisoners, to the number of thirty thousand soldiers of the military service of the United States, held as prisoners of war at Andersonville, the charge of murder being retained.

The specifications include the most cruel acts of barbarism. Judge Hughes spoke of these proceedings—arraigning the prisoner on a new list of charges, &c., without given counsel due notice, as extraordinary, and asked that additional time be given to enable the prisoner to prepare for his defense. This was granted, and the court adjourned until to-morrow noon. The counsel for Wirz have retired counseling. They have done all they could for him under the circumstances.

SECOND DISPATCH.

WASHINGTON, Aug. 23, 1865.

The Wirz military commission met this A. M. at 11 o'clock, at the Court of Claims room at the Capitol. Judge Hughes, counsel for accused, said, that as the prisoner should be brought into Court, he would would submit a motion. Maj. Gen. Wall remarked that time enough will be given for that purpose, Judge Hughes—I will present your case at the earliest moment. The prisoner was ot this stage of the proceedings brought into court in the custody of a military guard. Judge advocate Chipman called the roll of members, all of whom answered to their names. He then read an order from the war department, dated 22d of Ausust, in substance that the militory commission which was to convene on the 30th inst., is, by order of the President of the United States dissolved, and then read another order dated yesterday, convening a special commission to assemble to-day at 11 o'clock, for the trial of Henry Wirz, and such other prisoners as may be brought before it, the detail of officers being the same as that of the previous commission.

Maj. O. O. Hasler has, on application of Col. Chipman to the proper authority, been appointed assistant judge advocate.

Judge advocate Chipman asked the prisoner, whether he had any objection to the members of the Court. Mr. Peck, of course said that there was none personally to the members. Judge advocates and the official reporters were then sworn, to the effect that an addition to an impartial duty they would not improperly disclose the secret proceedings and sentence of the Court.

Judge Advocate Chipman, addressing the prisoner, said: "You are charged under the name of Henry Wirz. Is that your name?"

The prisoner said it was.

Judge Advocate Chipman—"The charges and specification will now be read."

Major General Wallace, the President of the Court—"Let the prisoner stand up."

Captain Wirz rose to his feet, when the charges and specifications were read. They are substantially the same as those upon which he was arraigned on Monday. He is first charged with maliciously, willfully and traitorously, and in aid of the then existing armed rebellion against the United States of America, on or before the first of March, 1864, and on divers other days between that day and the 10th day of April, 1865, combining, confederating and conspiring, together with John H. Winder, Richard B. Winder, Joseph White, W. S. Winder, R. R. Stevenson and others unknown, to injure the health and destroy the lives of soldiers in the military service of the United States, then held and being prisoners of war within the lines of the so-called confederate states, and in the military prisons thereof, to the end that the armies of the United States might be weakened and impaired in violation of the laws and customs of war.

The above differs from the former charges in this, namely, that the names of Robert E. Lee, James A· Seddon and Lucius D. Northrop are omitted. The other charges are that of murder, produced by heartless, brutal and cruel cruel treatment.

The specifications are fourteen in number. Judge advocate Chipman asked the prisoner what answer he had to make to the charge. The prisoner gave no reply. Judge Hughes, of counsel, said that these new charges or specifications, or the fact that any amendments or changes had been made in those heretofore presented, reached him now for the first time. The counsel had received an official note this morning from the judge advocate, which he would read, accompanied by a copy, as he supposed, of these charges. The note was received at eight o'clock or a little sooner, this morning, addressed to the firm of which he was a member, viz., Hughes, Denney & Peck, dated August 23, 1865.

The note from Judge advocate Chipman, is in substance briefly as follows :

"I enclose a copy of the charges and specifications with such changes as may be presented to-morrow. It is proper to say now what could not be said sooner, viz : The Court will assemble to-morrow at 11 o'clock in the Court of Claims' room, and I will proceed without delay with the case. The objections made by you will in part be removed by the orders of to-morrow, and there remains but two points to be raised by you to be settled. First, as to the jurisdiction of the Court, and second, as to the immunity of Capt. Wirz's claims under the arrangement with Capt. Noyes, and the capitulation as concluded, and between Johnston and Sherman. These I hope, will be disposed of to-morrow, or as soon as we get into the evidence."

Judge Hughes said the note was not dated yesterday, but to-day, this being the 23d.

Judge Advocate Chipman said the note was written yesterday, but was wrongly dated in the hurry.

Judge Hughes remarked that he saw by a morning paper only that the court was to meet to-day, and it was mere accident that he came here. The authorities were ample that the prisoner should have time to plead and prepare for defence, and to consult counsel; and on the prisoner's behalf he asked the commission to give him sufficient time. The prisoner, without any fault of his, would now be under the necessity of employing new counsel, as he, Judge Hughes was counsel, and as he, Judge Hughes, was inclined to think that he had rendered all the professional service required by his obligation, it was necessary for him to give the reasons for withdrawing from the case, but this ought not to prevent the court from determining the question of giving further time.

Judge Advocate Chipman did not object to his note being read, as an official paper. He placed the amendments to the charges in the hands of the counsel as soon as posible. The note was written at dark and sent by an old and faithful orderly and delivered at the office, which he supposed the gentleman occupied during the day, but they might have been out at the time. He had nothing to say against a proper adjournment to enable the prisoner to prepare for defence. He should certainly part from the gentleman with regret, yet he did not feel that either himself or the court ought to be intimidated by the threats of counsel. If there was any hard grievance he supposed the court would proceed properly and legally. He proposed to curtail no right or cut off any privilege to which counsel are entitled. He left the question of postponement to the court.

Judge Hughes remarked that this was a new court brought into being. The court would not subject the prisoner to the disadvantages of the reorganization of the court, and deny him the benefits which might result from it. This court knew nothing of the other or former charges. If he had said anything calculated to intimidate the court as intimated by the Judge Advocate, he was not aware of it. Even had he been so disposed, he would have had an admonition in the countenances of the officers composing the court, and the past conduct of those gentlemen, that it would be labor lost. They had been in the smoke of battle. Perhaps he would make a similar remark applicable to his friend, the Judge Advocate, if he was aware that the latter had ever been in battle, but he had not heard of it.

Mr. Peck, one of the counsel for the defence, suggested to the court that the recent action would bring up an entirely new class of defence, and would necessarily take up more time.

Judge Hughes here took up his hat, and placing a pile of law books under his arm, walked out of the court room. Mr. Peck resuming said, as the prisoner had once been arraigned and his life placed in jeopardy, he was entitled now either to an acquittal or trial on the former charges. He believed that all the authorities—civil and military—were conclusive on the point that if not acquitted the prisoner under the circumstances was entitled to all the benefits of an acquital.

The President of the court inquired of Mr. Peck whether he was still here in relation of counsel.

Mr. Peck replied that he was not.

The President said the Judge Advocate was here as the counsel of the defendant, the gentleman and his associates having withdrawn. Judge Advocate Chipman said, as the responsibility now attached to him of appearing for the prisoner, he asked an adjournment till to-morrow. He was unmindful of the rights of the prisoner. He regretted the retiring of the counsel. Judge had left on record the remark that he made no allusion to him as a soldier, not being aware that he had been in battle. In reply to this, he merely referred to the official records on file in the War Department. The commission adjourned until twelve o'clock to-morrow.

With regard to the charges and specifications against Capt. Wirz both Mr. Anderson and Mr. William C. Pitt the author of the map accompanying this work agree that in the main they are true, but as to specification No. 1, they have no personal knowledge. They neither have any doubt as to the will and intention of Wirz to do such a deed, but they regard him as too great a coward to perpetrate the act.

THE PRISONER WIRZ—HIS APPEARANCE IN COURT.

The appearance of Wirz, on his trial is thus described in the Philadelphia Inquirer:

" Wirz is a middle-aged man, apparently between forty-five or fifty years of age, about five feet eight inches high, of thin, spare figure, dark hair, whiskers and moustache, slightly tinged with gray. He has a high forehead, long nose, a keen piercing, dark eye, which wanders restlessly around the room and his action betokens a quick, nervous temperament.

He looked ill at ease, careworn and hurried. He was dressed in a black cloth coat and pantaloons, with white shirt, collar turned down, *a la* Byron, over a thick, heavy black silk neckerchief. His head gear consisted of a well worn, greasy-looking old silk hat, and this, with his seedy looking, thread-bare clothes, gave him a shabby genteel appearance.

He appears to take intense interest in the proceedings, sitting cross-legged, with his right hand constantly to his mouth, pulling his moustache with his thumb and forefingers in a nervous, agitated manner He evidently appreciates the solemnity of his situation.

His counsel conversed with him frequently, but his answers seem to be given mechanically and in monosyllables, in a low tone.

When the Court room was being cleared, he was taken into the lobby, and as he passed out, the spectators crowded around him for a moment, and one or two soldiers said, 'how are you, Wirz?' as if wishing to get him to recognize them. The guard promptly prevented any one coming near him or speaking to him, but he seemed to have an instinctive dread of the spectators, for he shrunk back and sought protection of the guard, as if he apprehended some violence being done him."

WILLIAM C. PITT'S HARDSHIPS ON THE MARCH.

Before proceeding with the Andersonville horrors, it will, perhaps, be proper to give some observations of Mr. W. C. Pitt, which did not come under the eye of Mr. Anderson for this reason, viz: although they were captured at the same time, they were sometimes separated; and while their general experience was very nearly the same, there were some occurrences on the march from Chicamauga to which Pitt was a separate witness.

After his capture, and while being guarded by the 26th Alabama to the rear, the woods were found to be on fire, and hundreds of dead and wounded were being consumed in the flames, shot and shell were flying in every direction, tree tops were being mowed down, and branches falling in every direction. One particular case came under Pitt's observation, which elicited his sympathy to the extreme. It was the case of a poor wounded soldier who was shot through the leg near the knee, and was so mangled that he could not help himself. The whole case is fully explained in the language of Mr. Pitt himself better than it could be done by any other person in the following words:

"One poor wounded man lay near a burning brush heap, and as I went by he called in a piteous tone to help him out of his agony; one foot was already burnt to a cinder; and I stooped down with the intention of relieving him from his misery; but as I was in the act of raising him from the devouring element, I heard the well known sound of the click of a gun; I looked around, and the guard had his musket raised and hammer cocked ready to fire, and said to me: 'You Yankee son of a b., let that man lay thar, or I'll be done shootin' a hole through you.' With regret I resumed my sad march for I preferred my life to certain death to both of us."

In going through Augusta, the people were very insulting,

particularly the women, who used all kinds of improper language, talking in a worse vernacular than Pitt had ever heard in his life, nor was this all they threw mud and missles of various kinds, and to cap the climax, threw the slops from their chamber windows at the prisoners. Their conduct became so furious and exceedingly bad, that the Col. who had charge of the prisoners, threatened that if they did not desist, he would turn the prisoners loose on the town. This had the effect to check them, but they still kept waving the rebel flag, and making wry faces and indicating their hostility, by various gestures, such as shaking their fists, putting their thumbs to their noses, and wagging the other digits in a contemptuous way.

At Smith's building Richmond, clothing and rations were sent from home. Such as the rebel authorities deemed proper were given the men in the line of clothing, but immediately a great many rebels were to be observed in new blue uniforms, it was natural to infer that our men did not get all that was sent. As to the rations the prisoners could see onions, potatoes, meat, coffee, crackers, sugar and besides a great supply of other things sent by the Sanitary Commission, carried into the building and could here hear the rebel guards opening the boxes at night. This was a general store house for all the prisoners in Richmond. Those confined in this building being aware of the great amount of stores, naturally enpected to get a supply, but were doomed to a sad disappointment. All that they received was three crackers per day for about five days, the balance of course went into rebels hands. From Smith's building, Richmond, Mr. Pitt and his fellow captives were taken to Danville.

At Danville these suffering men were placed in prison No. 5, where they were subjected to all kinds of hardship and insult. The prison was a tobacco factory and the men were placed on the different floors. Pitt and his fellows being on the third. There were 1,400 in all, distributed so as to occupy the four stories of the house. The small pox broke out at such a rate that from thirty to fifty patients were carried out on some days to the small pox hospital. The order came to vacinate all the prisoners, the work was immediately begun and prosecuted with vigor. Pitt declined going through the operation. The vaccination produced large sores on the arms of the victims, and after a time many had to have the vaccinated arm amputated to save their lives.

At this place about one hundred prisoners made their escape by tunnelling they got access to the cellar and commenced their operations and pretty soon they had a finished tunnel to a point behind a fence and beyond the guards.

When the rebs ascertained the escape of these men, they ordered those on the first floor to the others above. They were already full to suffocation, but that made no difference. The rebs seemed to think that their prison was like an omnibus, and could always take in a few more : So these poor fellows were crowded and packed together, and a strong guard was placed at the foot of the stairway to prevent any further attempt at escape.

This poor packed miserable crowd of men were kept until the next day towards evening without food or water, and without the privilege of going to the sinks! The horrible condition of the case can be imagined, but it is too revolting to describe.

Pitt, in going through all these hardships, got reduced almost to a skeleton. His usual weight is about 160 pounds, and this was his weight when he was captured at Chicamauga. What a change after his long sufferings on the march and in the various prisons! He happened to get a chance of being weighed at the company's quarters in Danville, and found his weight to be 83 pounds, or about his usual weight! Can any fact however presented give a more striking illustration of the hardships and sufferings of the unfortunates who had the ill fortune to be reduced to the condition of a prisoner of war in the so-called Southern Confederacy? Pitt had no disease, chronic or ortherwise. He is a strong able-bodied man, with an iron constitution, and was never sick one hour in prison, or during the whole term of his service in the Union army. Pitt's condition at this time was wholly attributable to the treatment he received and the hardships imposed on him in the way of hard marching, short rations, inadequate shelter, want of rest, close confinement, &c.

FURTHER PRACTICAL EXPERIENCE AND OBSERVATION AT ANDERSONVILLE.

The prisoners had heard of Camp Sumter, or the Andersonville prison to which they were destined, and of course human nature on such an occasion must give way to some feelings and emotions. These men in passing into the gates in many cases experienced the same emotions that in other times victims felt in passing the "Bridge of Sighs" in Venice. And the supperless and sleepless nights in the heavy dew without shelter, added the their first anxieties with regard to the horrors of their situation. The morning view of matters and things around them did not serve to dispel, but to increase these anxieties. They found themselves in a pen called a prison containing at that time about 20 dens. This pen was subsequently enlarged to the proportion shown by the map.

The next thing was to find out their true condition and circumstances. The first thing to which their attention was called was the dead line. This was a line marked by stakes being driven into the ground, and a rough extension of railing, the whole being only three or four feet high. They soon learned their position with regard to that line all of which is fully explained in the official charges against Capt. Wirz. It may as well be remarked however that many a poor fellow getting tired of starvation and the miseries surrounding, and preferring his chances in another world to the misires of their condition committed the act of *Felo de se* by getting himself to or beyond the limits of the dead line; which was certain to bring about his object, for the guards never failed to kill a man thus situated. or if they did not, failed in the attempt. It was well understood that any guard on duty, who killed a prisoner at the dead line would receive favors from head-quarters. He could demand and receive a furlough of from ten to thirty days at once.

Fifteen feet from the dead line, and enclosing it was the inner stockade as represented on the map. This was about seventeen feet high, and was constructed of square pine timbers inserted into the ground end wise to the distance of about six feet, and were placed as colse as possible.

On the outside and attached to this stockade were twenty-two stoops or platforms placed at a convient distance from each other and elevated to a sufficient height to command a perfect view of the dead line and of the whole camp. These were the sentry stands and were reached by stairs on the outside. Another stockade enclosed the one above described and was built in the same manner with round logs. It was was from 12 to 14 feet high and fifteen rods distant.

A third constructed in about the same style as the second. but only the eight feet high, enclosed the second at a distance of about 40 feet.

The fortifications were outside the stockades, and in position and shape as represented on the map. A glance at the works was sufficient to destroy nearly every vestage of hope of escape the captives naturally turned their attention to the condition of things more closely surrounding them.

The first thing attracting their attention was the fact that they were under the greatest general of the rebel army, namely General Starvation: and the first morning after meeting with Captain Wirz they began to learn more of that being, and found out pretty nearly what mercy would be received at his hands. He rode in on his inevitable grey mare, and called out: "Now you find out, poys, who Captain Wirz is; now you fall in quick, or I give you no preakfast!"

They fell in, but not before Captain Wirz had a chance to draw his revolver, and threaten several men in a most insulting manner, and the rations were distributed. The consisted for each man of a pint of corn meal and four ounces of meat. The corn meal was made from corn and cob ground together, and after all it was not so well ground that it was not unusual to find whole grains of corn in the meal. The men had nothing to cook their provisions in. They mixed the meal with water, and pasted it on a chip of wood, or anything they could find to answer their purpose, and baked it before the fire.

The next misery was that although timber is an encumberance to the ground in all that region, they could not procure enough, even if they had cooking utensils to do the cooking properly. The reason of the scantiness of wood grew out of the fact that a sufficient number of men were never detailed to get an ample supply.

The serious question in the minds of the prisoners was as to how long they could survive on such rations. With a great many that question was soon solved. Every morning the dead wagon came in to carry off those who had expired the preceeding night. The dead wagon that carried out the corpses came back loaded with corn meal or meat for rations. The captives who had been in the pen for two months previous to the arrival of Pitt were mere skeletons or shadows of men, very ragged and were as black as negroes. The blackness came from sitting close to their pine wood fires, the scantiness of wood making it necessary to retain but very small fires and the weather being so cold that it was necessary to get close to or over the fire to prevent freezing; furthermore they had no soap to wash off the accumulating blackness. The union soldier thus situated could be fully justified in repeating the lines of John Keats.

"My spirits lamp is faint and weak,
My feeble senses bow,
Death's finger pales my fading cheek,
His seal is on my brow.

My heart is as a withered leaf,
Each fibre dead and sere,
And near me sits the Spector grief,
To drain each burning tear.

The earth is bright with buds and bees,
The air with purple beams,
The winds are swimming in the trees,
Or sporting on the streams.

But not for me the blossoms breath,
Nor winds nor sunny skies,
I languish in the arms death,
And feed my soul with sighs.

It is not that I fear to die,
That burns my withered brow,
But thus to waste with agony,
And sigh and wish for rest."

CAPT. WIRZ AND HIS BLOODHOUNDS.

The prisoners soon began to learn more of the horrors by which they were surrounded and prominent among them was the fact that if they made their escape from the stockade they would be hunted down by bloodhounds kept for that purpose. These hounds were owned by a man by the name of Turner, who lived and kennelled his hounds at a distance of from 80 to 100 rods from the outer stockade.

They numbered 15 to 20 in the pack more or less owing to circumstances. Some of them being owned by the rebel Surgeons, and were only hired to Turner by the term, and when their owners did not want to use them for sporting purposes, but at all times Turner had a sufficient number to answer his fiendish purposes. Every morning Turner took his hounds and patrolled around the camp, taking a circle of about two miles from the camp for the purpose of finding a fresh track. If one was found, the hounds immediately followed. The only escape for the prisoner from being torn or mangled by the hounds was to climb a tree, and then his case was not better, the whole depending entirely upon the frame of mind that Mr. Turner might be in upon his arrival for if he was irritated at the length of time or trouble of catching the runaway, or for any other cause he would after the man descended, set the dogs on him and let them bite and tear the victim until his wrath was appeased, he did not allow the hounds to kill the man for that reason that when he delivered him alive he received thirty dollars " per head."

On these excursions in the morning. Capt. Wirz very frequently accompanied Turner, andit was remarkable that he did so when there was a pretty "sure thing" in finding game. Capt. Wirz remained the same stern inflexible man, the same identical character during the whole time of his administration. He rode the identical gray mare, and carried the same old revolvers from beginining to end. When he had caught a fugitive he never varied from his rule of putting him in the stocks. It may be as well to describe the stocks that were used before proceeding any further. They were made of planks and so constructed that in the day time a man confined in them would be compelled to stand all day, his neck being placed in a hole in two planks just large enough to receive it. At night his legs were placed each one through a hole similar to the one his neck had been during the day. At night the confined man had to remain on his back, not being able to change his position. Just at this point in writing of this narrative, the following was handed to me. It is from the Daily Wisconsin of Milwaukee, and has the stamp on its face of genuineness. the Wisconsin does not say where it it came from, but as other printed statements have been admitted in this work. Wirz, own statement, of course could not in any sense of fairness be omitted. His letter is as follows :

WIRZ' ACCOUNT OF HIMSELF.

ANDERSONVILLE, GA., May 7, 1865.

It is with great reluctance that I address you these lines, being fully aware how little time is left you to attend to such matters as I now have the honor to lay before you. I am a native of Switzerland, and was before the war a citizen of Louisiana, by profession a physician. Like hundreds and thousands of others, I was carried away by the malestrom of excitement and joined the Southern army. I was very seriously wounded at the battle of the Seven Pines near Richmond, Va., and have nearly lost the use of my right arm. Unfit for field duty, I was ordered to report to Brevet General John H. Winder, in charge of Federal prisoners of war, who ordered me to take charge of a prison in Tuscaloosa, Ala.

My health failing me, I applied for a furlough and went to Europe, from whence I returned in February, 1864; I was then ordered to report to the commandant of the military prison at Andersonville, Ga., who assigned me to the command of the interior of the prison. The duties I had to perform were arduous and unpleasant, and am satisfied that no man can or will blame me for things that happened here, and which were beyond my power to control. I do not think that I ought to be held responsible for the shortness of rations, for the overcrowded state of the prison, which was in itself a prolific source of the fearful mortality, for the inadequate supplies of clothing, want of shelter, &c., &c.; still I now bear the odium, and men who were prisoners here seem disposed to wreak their vengeance upon me for what they have suffered, who was only the medium, or, I may better say, the tool in the hands of my superiors This is my condition; I am a man with a family; I lost all my property when the Federal army besieged Vicksburg; I have no money at present to go any place, and even if I had I know of no place where I could go; my life is in danger, and I most respectfully ask of you help and relief. If you will be so generous as to give me some sort of a safe conduct, or what I should greatly prefer a guard to protect myself and family against violence, I shall be thankful to you, and you may rest assured that your protection will not be given to one who is unworthy of it. My intention is to return with my family to Europe as soon as I can make the arrangements. In the meantime, I have the honor, General, to remain, very respectfully, your obedient servant, H. Y. WIRZ, Captain C. S. A.

Major General J. H. Wilson, United States Army, commanding Macon, Georgia.

This letter admits the whole case of the suffering and is all summed up in the single sentence of Capt. Wirz's letter. "I do not think that I ought to be held responsible for the shortness of rations for the overcrowded state of the prison which was in itself a prolific source of fearful mortality for the inadequate supplies of clothing, want of shelter, &c., &c."

This sentence means and contains a very large amount of useful information from a proper source. It is from the man in charge of this channel house. It was indeed a fearful mortality. Thirteen thousand of our patriotic soldiers sleep their last sleep in the trenches called the burying ground of this modern Golgatha. The life of each one of these departed men was of as much consequence to him as that of Jeff Davis is to to him, or that of Capt. Wirz, is now to himself in this hour of tribulation. Capt. Wirz does not inform who is responsible.

"Double, double toil and trouble,
"Fire burn and cauldron bubble."

Heretofore the men had been calculating how long they were to live or rather how soon starvation would end their miseries, when a new trouble arose. Detachments of additional prisoners arrived every few days until the number amounted to about 20,000 in the stockade before its enlargement. It at this time contained about twenty-two acres. It now became a serious question as to how soon they were to be suffocated. The crowd was so great that it became impossible to call the roll. At least 7,000 or about one third of the whole number had no kind of shelter, neither had they blankets. They slept in the streets or wherever they could get a resting place. To add to the misery in the already sufficiently bad state of things in June there was about twenty-four days of incessant rain. Of course the dead wagons had plenty of business. They began their business early in the morning and continued it generally nearly all day.

There was what was called a hospital on the outside, but not one quarter of the exhausted sick and dying could get to it. Every morning men were found dead in the crowded stockade, and were carted off to their final resting place. It was now with the men, a question as to whether they were doomed to starvation by a slow process, or to die by suffocation in the crowded pen. One or the other seemed inevitable sooner or later. Vermin abounded to such an extent that they impregnated the sand through the whole camp. The soil is one continued bed of sand. A person could take up a handful of sand and place it in the sun on a shingle, and pretty soon the quantity would be diminished by the creeping out of these pests. The one making the experiment need not go to any particular locality, but could arrive at the same results in any portion of the pen. It was remarked before, that in June there were 24 days rain. In this continued storm, a portion of the stockade at the creek which passes through the pen, washed away, affording quite a chance of escape, but no one availed himself of it. The reason was, every one was so weak, drenched and emaciated that there was no courage or ambition left. About the first day of July, the Stockade was enlarged to the dimensions represented on the map, but prisoners still kept pouring in until the number was swelled to thirty-two thousand. So the case was not made so much better as at first glance might be imagined. In fact, it every day grew worse from the accumulation of filth.

No shelter was given the men in the way of tents or otherwise and the only protection from the rays of the burning sun, was afforded to the lucky few who by hook or by crook retained their blankets, these were managed by Yankee ingenuity to be converted into some kind of protection against the heat and cold, but a very large majority of the prisoners had not even this poor comfort. They had been robbed of their blankets by orders from high authority. The suffering grew more intense day by day, each succeeding day making matters worse. The water which was none too good at the outset became day by day more filthy, and the creek called Sweet Creek had become so outrageously filthy that it was scarcely fit to bath in. This Sweet Creek passes through the camp as represented on the map, and besides the washings of filth from the stockade received before entering it, the washings of filth from the rebel camp above.

After awhile the prisoners conceived the idea of digging wells, but they had no shovels or other implements usually used for such purposes, still they managed to dig wells. They used portions of used up canteens or any other implement that would scoop up the earth. Of course the wells were produced by an immense amount of labor and the exercise of unexampled patience.

They succeeded in this way in getting purer water, but the filth and malaria was increasing from day to day and the list of mortality increased in a corresponding ratio. During the months of July, August and September the deaths numbered between two and three thousand per month. Fifty men were constantly employed in digging the burial trenches and burying the dead, or rather covering them up, it cannot be called a christian burial. The trenches were four feet deep, seven feet wide, and 160 feet long, with a direction East and West. In these trenches the corpses were placed, their bodies being in a North and South direction, over one hundred being placed in one trench, the heads being placed to the North. When the bodies were thrown into the trenches in rather a careless manner, the next thing was to cover them up, and then the next business was to place head boards, but as these were placed at equal distances after the trenches had been filled, it would be very questionable whether a relative of the deceased who sought to re-inter at home the remains of his martyred friend would get the right body or not.

But to think of the appalling mortality when it was in its extreme in July, August and September, and reduce it to a practical view is perfectly astounding. Some place it as high as 3,000 per month, others at 2,000 and over.

The grounds in which thsese victims were confined were hardly enough unobstructed to give a school boy his morning exercises. They contained only about 40 acres of land; now if the extreme number of deaths be taken as the guide, then in round numbers there were carried from this small pen and the adjacent hospital one hundred bodies per day. The minimum makes the number sixty-six.

Any city in christendom showing one half that mortality in proportion to the number of inhabitants would be deserted by the entire population in three days. In this case however there was no chance of escape, and the poor victims could only remain and be witnesses to the horrible scenes around them, and each one "bide his time."

As to the departed heroes who were thus sacrificed or tortured to death, merely because they served their country faithfully and became martyrs on the altar of their country, its constitution and laws, they were doubtless immediately more happy on their departure for "that undiscovered country from whose bourne no traveller returns" than thosewho were compelled to remain and suffer. Could not the departing men with **propriety adopt the language of Mozart in his requiem.**

" Spirit, thy labor is o'er,
Thy term of probation is gone,
Thy steps are now bound for the untrodden shore.
And the race of immortals begun.

Spirit! look not on the strife
Of pleasures of earth with regret—
Pause not on the threshold of limitless life,
To mourn for the day that is set.

Spirit! no fetters can bind,
No wicked have power to molest:
There the weary, like thee, the wretched shall find
A haven—a mansion of rest.

Spirit! how bright is the road
For which thou art now on the wing!
Thy home it will be with thy Savior and God,
Their loud hallelujahs to sing."

LIST OF WISCONSIN SOLDIERS WHO DIED AT ANDERSONVILLE, GEORGIA.

36 G W Forducy, private, company C, 7th Wis., March 12, 1864, dysentery.
68 J J Schleason, Corp., company F, 7th Wis., March 19, 1864, dysentery.
303 Carl Helt, private, company E, 26th Wis., April 2, 1864, dysentry.
440 H. Shrigley, private, company G, 10th Wis., April 8, 1864, diarrhea.
603 J Palmer, Corporal, company C, 7th Wis., April 17, 1864, diarrhea.
710 A C Hale, private, company I, 21st Wis., April 24, 1864, Feb. Typ.
884 P Winters, private, company M, 1st Cav., May 5, 1864, diarrhea.
929 A C Webster, Sergeant, company E, 7th Inf., May 7, 1864, bronchitis.
1002 J Haskins, private, company E, 1st Inf., May 10, dysentery.
1009 J Walder, private, company F, 1st Cav., May 10, 1864, chronic diarrhea.
1165 J Kummilt, private, company H, 1st Inf., May 17, 1864, diarrhea.
1260 C W Fuller, Corporal, company E, 7th Inf., May 21, 1864, chronic diarrhea.
1341 H Bowen, private, company A, 1st Inf., May 24, dysentery.
1529 O Gilbert, Sergeant, company K, 10th Inf., June 1, 1864, diarrhea.
1591 E Duffey, private, company L, 1st Cav., June 3, 1864, diarrhea.
1605 H H Hoffland, Sergeant, company K, 15th Inf., June 5, 1864, diarrhea.
1752 J Mangen, Corporal, company H, 24th Inf., June 8, 1864, anasarca.
1838 O Bush, private, company B, 15th Inf., June 11, 1864, Feb. Typ.

1896 J Milligan, private, company B, 1st Inf., June 13, 1864, diarrhea.
1909 M S Welton, private, company L, 1st Cav., June 13, 1864, diarrhea.
2003 — Jacobson, Corporal, company D, 15th Inf., June 15, 1864, diarrhea.
2055 H Bail, private, company A, 7th Wis., June 16, 1864, scurvy.
2113 J R Alewynes, private, company E, 24th Wis., June 18, 1864, scurvy.
2128 H A Bowhan, Sergt., company F, 10th Wis., June 18, 1864, anasarca.
2148 S W Turney, private, company D, 21st Wis., June 18, 1864, diarrhea.
—— A Ronch, private, company F, 21st Wis., June 18, 1864, diarrhea.
2283 W H Fountain, private, company A, 16th Inf., June 21, 1864, diarrhea.
2309 J S Uppell, private, company B, 15th Inf., June 22, 1864, dysentery.
2344 E Brooks, private, company H, 1st Cav., June 22, 1864, dysentery.
2360 A Church, private, company H, 7th Inf., June 23, 1864, scurvy.
2384 J Hanson, private, company K, 15th Inf., June 23, 1864, scurvy.
2385, T Fay, private, company K, 1st Inf., June 24th, 1864, dysentery.
2393 F Grash, private, combany I, 10th Inf., June 24, 1864, dysentery.
2419 J Enger, private, company F, 15th Inf., June 24th, 1864, diarrhea.
2457 C F Boomer, Corp., company I, 10th Inf., June 24, 1864, diarrhea.
2498 J Knudson, private, company E, 15th Inf., June 26, 1864, diarrhea.
2522 E Dambrochler, private, company I, 26th Inf., June 26, 1864, diarrhea.
2535 A Plum, private, company K, 4th Cav., June 26th, 1864, diarrhea.
2536 B F Hough, Corp., company K, 10th Inf., June 27, 1864, dysentery.
2588 R Tomlinson, private, company D, 6th Inf., June 28, 1864, dysentery.
2591 G Winchester, private, company I, 21st Inf., June 28, 1864, scurvy.
—— S B Waller, private, company G, 21st Inf., June 17, 1864, diarrhea.
2663 J Chapman, private, company G, 2d Inf., June 29, 1864, diarrhea.
2681 O Broms, private, company G, 15th Inf., June 30, 1864, diarrhea.
2732 W McMan, private, company G, 3d Battery, July 1, 1864, diarrhea.
2817 R. Stiffer, private, company F, 15th Inf., July 8, 1864, dysentery.
2847 A Peterson, Corp., company K, 15th Inf., July 3, 1864, diarrhea
2951 E McCormich, private, company L, 1 Cav., July 6, 1864, dysentery.
2954 O H Vohost, private, company L, 1 Cav., July 6, 1864, diarrhea.
2969 D Cowles, private, company B, 10 Inf., July 6, 1864, bronchitis.
3009 P Lack, private, company A, 7th Inf., July 7, 1864, diarrhea.
3076 J Vetter, private company F, 6th Inf., July 9, 1864, diarrhea.
3078 F. Sirbert, private, company C, 24th Inf. July 9, 1864, diarrhea.
3120 D D Thompson private, company 36th Inf., July 9, 1864, dysentery,
3162 O Oleson, private, company B, 15th Inf., July 11, 1864, diarrhea.
3164 H Guth, private, company D, 1st Inf., July, 11, 1864, diarrhea.
3244 J Daygo, private, company L, 1st. Cav. July 13, 1864, bronchitis.
8253 J Brown, private, company H, 4th Cav., July 13, 1764, pneumonia.
3292 S Cummings, private, company A, 21st Inf,, July 14, 1864, diarrhea.

3375 J Tyler, Corp., company A, 10th Inf., July, 16, 1864, chronic diarrhea.
3878 Charles Went, private, company B, 7th Inf., July 16, 1864, diarrhea.
3390 D Greenman, Sergt., company K, 21st Inf, July 16, 1864, dysentery.
3503 W Shoop, private, company G, 1st Wis., July 18, 1864, diarrhea.
3511 J B Pickett, Corp., company F, 1st Wis., July 18, 1864, diarrhea.
3583 J Sutton, private, company E, 10th Wis., July 19, 1864, diarrhea.
3624 H Beuseler, private, company G, 2d Wis., July 20, 1864 diarrhea.
3645 Chas McSanlin private, company I, 36th Wis., July 20, 1864 diarrhea.
3661 C P Tucker, private, company I, 1st Wis., July 20, 1864, diarrhea.
3665 F S Reynolds, private, company K, 10th Wis., July 20, 1864, dysentery.
3673 Henry Bruce, private, company H, 24th Wis., July 20, 1864, diarrhea.
3720 O Henderson, private, company F, 15th Wis., July 21, 1864, typhoid fever.
3828 R Crane, Drummer, company D, 7th Wis., July 23, 1864, diarrhea.
4133 Jas B Kellett, Corp., company B, 21st Wis., July 28, 1864, intermittent fever.
4289 K Nelson, private, company K, 15th Wis., July 30, 1864, scurvy.
4340 M Pardy, private, company E, 10th Wis., July 30, 1864, diarrhea.
4343 J W Sharp, private, company G, 2d Wis., July 30, 1864, diarrhea.
4378 W H Smith, private, company B, 10th Wis., July 31, 1864, scurvy.
4390 C Chapel, private, company E, 1st Inf., June 31, 1864, chronic diarrhea.
4405 L Kull, private, company C, 24th Inf., June 31, 1834, chronic diarrhea.
4436 J Shun, private, company H, 24th Inf., June 30, 1864, diarrhea.
4467 A L Taylor, private, company E, 25th Inf., Aug. 1, 1864, diarrhea.
4477 Isaac Austin, private, company G, 25th inf., Aug. 1, diarrhea.
4542 Nelson, private, company B, 10th Inf., Aug. 2, 1864, scurvy.
4570 F Halts, private, company C, 26th Inf., Aug. 26, 1864, scurvy.
4614 C W Kellips, private, company E, 1st Cav , Aug. 3, 1864, scurvy.
4706 D Wakefield, private, company K, 25th Inf., Aug. 4, 1864, diarrhea.
4783 E G Scott, Sergt., company D, 21st Inf., Aug. 5, 1864, diarrhea.
4882 John Slingerlaw, private, company L, 1st Cav., Aug. 6, 1864, diarrhea.
4925 E H Matherson, private, company E, 2d Inf., Aug. 6, 1864, diarrhea.
4890 M S Northam, Sergt, Company C, 10th Inf., Aug. 7, 1864, diarrhea.
4997 G. Reed, private, company K, 1st Inf , Aug. 7, 1864, dysentery.
5007 W K Forslay, private, company K, 8th Inf., Aug. 8, 1864, scurvy.
5026 H Briggs, private, company C, 1st Cav., Aug. 8, 1864, dysentery.
5042 J Murray, private, company D, 24th Inf., Aug. 8, 1864, diarrhea.
5100 John Budson, private, company L, 1st Cav., August 9, 1864, scurvy.
5102 John Cavenough, private, company H, 1st Inf., Aug. 9, 1864, scurvy.
5241 A Abbott, Sergeant, company D, 1st Inf., Aug. 10, 1864, scurvy.

5312 F B Howard, private, company K, 10th Inf., Aug. 10, 1864, pleurisy.
5322 E Briggs, private, company L, 1st Cav., Aug. 11, 1864, scurvy.
5397 J N Livingston, private, company E, 3rd Art., Aug. 12, 1864, anasar.
5453 C B Allen, private, company G, 2nd Inf., Aug. 12, vul slop.
5472 Geo Angler, private, company F, 10th Inf., Aug. 13, 1864, scurvy.
5557 M Greenwall, private, company C, 1st Cav., Aug. 13, 1864, dysentery.
5564 W Bailey, Corporal, company E, 25th Inf., Aug. 13, 1864, vul sclop.
5628 A Holenbach, private, company D, 25th Inf., Aug. 14, 1864, vul sclop.
5683 P Morries, private, company D, 10th Inf., Aug. 15, 1864, scurvy.
5739 Henry Main, private, company F, 30th Inf., Aug. 15, 1864, diarrhea.
5759 Oscar Fluno, private, company H, 1st Cav., Aug. 15, 1864, diarrhea.
5792 J Rassmusson, private, company L, 1st Cav., Aug. 15, 1864, dysentery.
5811 J B Fish, Sergeant, company H, 1st Cav., Aug. 16, 1864, dirrrhea.
5830 Fred Destler, private, company G, 24th Inf., Aug. 16, 1864, diarrhea.
6088 Wm Robinson, Corporal, company C, 10th Inf., Aug. 18, 1864, scurvy.
6090 Wm. Nichols, private, company I, 10th Inf., Aug. 18, 1864, dysentery.
6097 D Frisnor, Sergt., company A, 36th Inf., Aug. 18, 1864, icturus.
6160 C Erickson, private company B, 16th Inf. Aug. 16, 1864, cerebritus.
6204 S Burrick, private, company I, 17th Inf., Aug. 20, 1864, scurvy.
6231 A McClury, private, company E, 10th Inf., Aug. 20, 1864, chronic diarrhea.
6236 Wm Farrow, private, company A, 1st Inf., Aug. 20, 1864, dysentery.
6377 F Messer, private, company K, 5th Inf., Aug. 21, 1865, scurvy.
6406 J. Pronis, private, company F, 17th Inf., Aug. 22, 1764, vul. sclop.
6418 C C Carrier, private, company F, 21st Inf., Aug. 22, 1764, vul. sclop.
6468 A W Hale, private, company I, 21st Inf., Aug. 22, 1864, diarrhea.
6614 John E Goom, private, company G, 36th Inf., Aug. 23, 1865, diarrhea.
6642 G Lansing, private, company A, 10th Inf., Aug. 23, 1864, scurvy.
6858 T Taylor, private, company E, 6th Inf., Aug. 26, 1864, Dysentery.
6938 J R Jermings, Corp., company G, 45th Inf., Aug. 26, 1864, diarrhea.
6943 E Starr, private, company F, 16th Inf., Aug. 26, 1864, vul. sclop.
6967 Bery Dich, private, company G, 36th Inf., July 27, 1864, scurvy.
7149 B Hutchings, private, company E, 1st Cav., July 29, 1864, diarrhea.
7160 P Thorn private, company L, 1st Cav., July 29, 1864, chronic diarrhea.
7235 F Lowe, private company G, 16th Inf., July 29, 1864, scurvy
7295 J Bailey, private, company I, 36th Inf., July 30, 1864, dysentery.
7323 J Burke, private, company E, 10th Inf., July 30, 1864, gangrene.
7355 L Gremds, private, company I, 15th Inf., July 31, 1864, chronic diarrhea.
7455 J F Davis, private, company B, 36th Inf., Sept., 1, 1864, diarrhea.
7522 M Lawson, private, company B, 15th Inf., Sept. 1, 1864, dysentery.
7530 J Pardy, private, company I, 10th Inf., Sept. 1, 1864, scurvy.

7614 M Seaman, Sergeant, company D, 21th Inf., Sept. 2, 1864, dysentery.
7649 L Hanson, private, company B, 15th Inf., Sept. 3, 1864, scurvy.
7755 E Bordon, Corp., company K, 21st Inf., Sept. 4, 1864, chronic diarrhea.
7759 P Boyle, private, company B, 25th Inf., Sept. 4, 1864, diarrhea.
7791 W H Harding, Sergeant, company C, 21st Inf, Sept. 4, 1864, scurvy.
7893 S Peterson, private, company K, 15th Inf., Sept. 5, 1864, scurvy.
8105 G M Chase, Corporal, company A, 1st Inf., Sept. 7, 1864, diarrhea.
8168 L Smith, private, company K, 4th Cav., Sept. 8, 1864, diarrhea.
8299 M O Kinds, private, company A, 21st Inf., Sept. 9, 1864, scurvy.
8326 D Group, private, company H, 4th, Cav., Sept. 10, 1864, Gangrene.
8359 H Vanscorter, private, company C, 1st Cav., Sept. 10, 1864, gangrene.
8427 J Vanderbilt, private, company D, 36th Inf., Sept. 11, 1864, scurvy.
8460 W B Farnham, private, company K. 4th Cav., Rept. 11, 1864, scurvy.
8500 A Frontman, private, company K, 2d Inf., Sept. 12, 1864, scurvy.
8515 A J Pillsberry, private, company H, 1st Cav., Sept. 12, 1894, gangrene.
8562 W Kendall, private, company E, 32d Inf., Sept. 12, 1864, diarrhea.
8576 J Batchellor, private, company I, 1st. Inf., Sept. 12, 1864, diarrhea.
8584 M High, private, company E, 25th Inf., Sept. 12, 1864, vul. sclop.
8587 A Depas, private, company A, 21st Inf., Sept. 12, 1864, dysentery.
8601 S Ellenwood, Sergt. company C, 10th Inf., Sept. 12, 1864, diarrhea.
8914 J Ingham., private, company K, 10th Inf. Sept. 12, 1864, scurvy.
8611 C C Bushu, Corp., company B, 2d Inf., Sept. 13, 1864, chronic diarrhea.
8564 J Patterson, private, company A, 21st Inf. Sept. 13, 1864, scurvy.
8592 A F Adams, private, company E, 36th Inf., Sept. 14, 1864, scurvy.
8944 F Lairch, private, company K, 26th Inf., Sept. 16, 1864, scurvy.
9014 H Pointer, Sergt., company F, 10th Inf., Sept. 17, 1864, diarrhea.
9073 Wm Kerreger, private, company G, 36th Inf, Sept. 17, 1854, diarrhea.
9169 G Carlentyre, private, company G, 23d Inf., Sept. 18. 1861, scurvy.
9333 D Haller, private, company D, 12th Inf., Sept. 20, 1864, scurvy.
9337 S Ericson, private, company D, 30th Inf., Sept. 20, 1864, dysentery.
9461 C Peterson, private, company I, 15th Inf., Sept. 21, 1864, scurvy.
9458 W B Woodward, private. company A, 1st Inf., Sept. 22, 1864, scurvy.
9607 J Blinknar, private, company A, 2d Inf., Sept. 23. 1864, scurvy.
9604 F Ferguson, Sergt., company A, 15th Inf., Sept. 24, 1864, diarrhea.
9693 M Snyder, private, company E, 26 Inf., Sept. 24, 1864, scurvy.
9739 G Dacy, private, company I, 12th Inf., Sept. 25th, 1864, diarrhea.
9808 A Irwin, private, company C., 25th Inf., Sept. 26th, 1864, scurvy.
9860 J Rice, private, company C, 7th Inf., Sept. 27, 1864, scurvy.
9802 S Patterson, Corp., company I, 15th Inf., Sept. 27, 1864, scurvy.
9938 J Wick, private, company H, 1st Cav., Sept. 28, 1864, diarrhea.
9997 E Latgur, private, company A, 15th Inf., Sept. 29, 1864, scurvy.

10213 E Willis, Corp., company E, 7th Inf., Oct. 2, 1864, scurvy.
10234 M Fagan, private, company G, 15th Inf., Oct. 2. 1864, diarrhea.
10289 S Myers, private, company I, 15th Inf., Oct. 4, 1864, scurvy.
10346 H Cronning, private, company C, 7th Inf., Oct. 5, 1864, scurvy.
10369 Wm Neff, private, company I. 32d Inf., Oct. 5, 1864, scurvy.
10395 F Winchel, private, company D, 17th Inf, Oct. 6, 1864, scurvy.
10427 P Hanes, private, company D, 10th Inf., Oct. 6, 1864, scurvy.
10536 F Keane, Corporal, company E, 26th Inf., Oct. 8 1864, diarrhea.
10685 H Britton, Sergeant, company B, 15th Inf., Oct. 11, 1864, scurvy.
10691 H Gunderson, Sergeant, company I, 15th Inf, Oct. 11, 1864, scurvy.
10692 H Knowles, private, company D, 21st Inf., Oct. 11, 1864, diarrhea.
10752 C Castle, private, company C, 1st Cav., Oct. 12, 1864, scurvy.
10771 John Davis, private, company B, 1st Inf., Oct. 12, 1864, scurvy.
10830 P Adams, private, company A, 10th Inf., Oct. 13, 1864, scurvy.
10919 N Robinson, private, company I, 15th Inf., Oct. 14, 1864, scurvy.
11020 W Coburne, private, company A, 10th Inf., Oct. 16, 1864, scurvy.
11037 S M Smith, Corporal, company F, 21st Inf., Oct. 17, 1864, scurvy.
11047 A D Sails, private, company K, 4th Cav., Oct. 17, 1864, scurvy.
11088 F Chusterson, private, company E, 15th Inf., Oct. 18, 1864, hemorhage.
11284 W H Johnson, private, company H, 6th Inf., Oct. 22, 1864, scurvy.
11236 D Thurber, Corp., company G, 36th Inf., Oct. 21, 1864, diarrhea
11323 H Worlfinger, private, company H, 12th Inf., Oct. 23, 1864, scurvy.
11399 F Voele, Corp., company E, 10th Inf., Oct. 24, 1864, scurvy.
11420 E B Tyler, private, company F, 10th Inf., Oct. 24, 1864, scurvy.
11443 C Holenbeck, private, company A, 13th Inf, Oct. 25, 1864, scurvy.
11475 P Thorson, private, company G, 24th Inf., Oct. 26t, 1864, scurvy.
11492 E V McArthy, Corpl., company E, 13th Inf., Oct. 26th, scurvy.
11535 J Chamberlain, private, company I, 21st Inf., Oct. 27, scurvy.
11545 F Ochle, private, company E. 26th Inf., Oct. 27, 1864, scurvy.
11610 L Batterson, private, company K, 10th Inf., Oct. 28th, 1864, diarrhea.
11687 P Ellenger, private, company K, 21st Inf., Oct. 31, 1864, chronic diarrhea.
11734 M Butler, private, company K. 10th Inf., Nov. 2, 1864, scurvy.
11744 W C. Clark, private, company C, 10th Inf., Nov. 2, 1864, scurvy.
11812 J Rattles, private, company D, 25th Inf., Nov. 4, 1864, scurvy.
11927 W Hanson, private, company B, 1st Inf., Nov. 8, 1864, scurvy.
11931 M Olston, private, company B, 15th Inf., Nov. 9, 1864, diarrhea.
11936 E Mulaskey, private, company B, 21st Inf., Nov. 9, 1864, scurvy.
12032 R Blakely, private, company F, 17th Inf., Nov 14, 1864, scurvy.
12111 M Whalen, private, company B, 12th Inf., Nov. 24, 1864, dysentery.
12167 N Harris, private, company D, 12th Inf., Nov. 26, 1864, dysentery.
12233 B Richmond, Sergt., company L, 1st Cav., Dec. 6, 1864, dysentery.

12242 P D Randall, private, company K, 1st Inf., Dec. 7, 1864, scurvy.
12286 H Enghert, private, company G, 36th Inf., Dec. 14, 1864, scurvy.
12468 G Hand, private, company D, 10th Inf., Jan. 16, 1864, gangrene.
12618 A Frost, private, company B. 7th Inf., Feb 8, 1864, gangrene.
12626 A Yessau, private, company A. 24th Inf., Feb. 10, 1864, scurvey.
12653 W R Forguson, private, company B, 24th Inf., 1864, diarrhea.
15728 —— Antone, private, company D, 31st Inf., March 4, 1864, diarrhea.
12750 D B David, private, company B, 25th Inf., March 8, 1864, gangrene.
——- A Denmark, private, company A, 1st Cav.
——- C. Merrill, private, company K, 4th Cav.
——- J Richlin, private, company D, 1st Cav., Dec. 26, 1864, dysentery.
——- J Rice, private, company C, 7th Inf.
——- J Harvey, private, company G, 1st Inf.
——- E S Hardy, Sergt., company E, 6th Inf., Feb. 4, 1864, diarrhea.
——- L B Cook, private, company C, 2d Cavalry.

The foregoing list shows in the language of Capt. Wirz, "a fearful mortality. It further shows that Wisconsin furnished her full quota of Victims.

These men of Wisconsin were tortured to death. In many cases in a manner too revolting to record. Who did this "deed without a name." One person intimately connected with the management of affairs there, as before stated, declares that he ought not to be held responsible, that he was a mere tool in the hands of others. The investigation now going on will probably develop the guilty parties.

The list of mortality of course does not show the full extent of Wisconsin calamity. Many of the prisoners not enumerated in the roll, (that being simply a list of the buried at Andersonville) died before they reached home. Many died pretty shortly after, many are now lingering out a miserable existence soon to end, and a large majority are more less constitutionally broken down. There is a fearful criminal responsibility resting somewhere which of course must soon be brought to light. Wisconsin in the name of her martyred sons will demand that the guilty parties be ferretted out and punished.

MORE ABOUT ANDERSONVILLE.

The prisoners had to resort to some occupation to pass away time, and it soon became necessary to establish some police regulations for this large population. Characters of every grade were to be found. It finally became necessary to establish courts of justice. In the way of occupation to pass away the weary hours, the men employed themselves in making from the beef bones, rings, toothpicks and trifles of ornament, all being done with no other instrument than the jack-knife, these were in great demand, the purchasers being confederates. A skillful workman could supply himself with tobacco and sundry other articles of necessity or convenience by the manufacture of these and other ornamental trinkets. There is an inborn disposition in the American character to trade, traffic and grow rich, or fail in the attempt. This characteristic, notwithstanding the forlorn condition of these unfortunates soon developed itself. Markets were established, barter commenced and pretty soon among these forlorn people quite a trade was established. It must not be understood that the successful business operator got rich in money. His highest ambition was to get an increased supply of provisions. The highest success attained by which the successful industrious speculator was to get enough to live upon.

The Northern Army has in its ranks men of all ranks, grades and profession. The Andersonville prisons were an illustration of this fact. If preaching was required a preacher was at hand. If a lawyer was wanted more than could be retained were instantly on hand.

This city of horrors had in its borders a fair representation of all classes of people. The christian gentlemen was to be found there, and from him down through grades and shades of character until pickpockets, thieves, robbers and murderers were included in the list of characters composing this community.

The last mentioned characters followed their professions to such an extent that they become objects of terror to the whole community. They soon become designated and known by the name of Raiders. They seemed to act in combination or separately as the case required. If any fellow prisoner was fortunate enough to save any valuable thing either in money or other personal property, these professionals seemed to find it out almost by instinct. The possesor of any valuable article was sure to become an object of interest to these precious scoundrels, and if he did not become a victim he might bless his own good fortuate. These men were experts. They had evidently plied their professions before entering the army. They manufactured instruments by which they could cut open a pocket without detection. They could relieve a man of his valuables in many cases without his knowledge while the victim was asleep, and if he (the victim) was awakened by the operation they knew how to silence him even if they had to go so far as murder. Their operations were finally carried to such an extent that they became objects requiring same combined action to relieve the camp of their depredation. These men were generally from large cities and at home would be known by the name of "Roughs." They numbered from one hundred and fifty to two hundred. When their conduct had become so notoriously outrageous that forbearances ceased to be a virtue, their case was taken in hand by their fellow prisoners.

The facts as far as ascertainable were collected and presented to Capt. Wirz who promptly arrested the culprits. A court was at once formed with judge and jury, which proceeded to try them. It has been stated on good authority that this court in point of ability would compare favorably with any other court possessing or assuming the same powers.

About 40 men were on trial. The proceedings were all in

regular form, and the case given the jury in the regular form. Then the verdict was given and the sentence followed. Some were sentenced to wear the ball and chain for ninety days and six were sentenced to hanged. The trial took place outside of the stockade and lasted three or four days. The condemned were in custody of Capt. Wirz. When the time come for the execution of the condemned, Capt. Wirz brought them under guard into the stockade and said, "Now poys you have tried these men by a jury of your own men, and a schudge of your own choosing, now you do schust what you please mit dem, and immediately left the grounds.

The result was that these men were shortly seen dangling between heaven and earth in accordance with the sentence of the court.

MR. PITT'S RELATION TO THE WITNESS HOGAN IN HIS TRIAL.

Pitt had the good fortune to be detailed as ward master in the general hospital, which to some extent relieved him of his miseries, and gave him opportunity to more minutely observe the progress of matters and things.

Martin E. Hogan, of Terre Haute, Indiana, of the 5th New York Cavalry, was chief steward. This brought him and Pitt in daily contact, and made them acquaintances and friends, and when Hogan finally made his escape Pitt became his successor in office.

The following testimony, which Hogan has given in the trial of Wirz, will show his effort to escape at that time, and with some explanations of the case by Pitt will present Mr. Hogan in the light of being a determined unflinching hero. His testimony in the court is as follows:

Martin E. Hogan testified as to his having been a prisoner

at Andersonville. The men there were in a miserable condition; as bad as possibly could be. As to hounds, he was brought back to prison by their agency. He had seen Captain Wirz with hounds trying to strike the track of an escaped prisoner for attempting to escape from prison about the 8th of October, 1864.

After the most obscene abuse from Captain Wirz he was fastened by the neck and feet, and remained there sixty-eight hours; he heard Wirz give orders that he should not have food, but he did get food from some paroled comrades who stole it for him. He had seen these comrades put in the stocks at the same time. One man was put in because he asserted his manhood by resenting the abuse of a confederate soldier. When the prisoners were being removed from Andersonville to Millen the witness saw Captain Wirz take a man by the collar because he could not walk faster. The man was so worn by disease that he could not walk. Throwing the man on his back, he stamped on him with his feet. He saw the man bleeding, and he died a short time after. In the dissecting room he saw students in the pursuit of knowledge sawing open the skulls of deceased prisoners and opening the bodies. When he escaped he took with him a knife to protect himself from harm if necessary. It was a confederate surgeon's knife which he had taken without leave. His companions who attempted to escape were provided with revolvers. Several rounds were fired at the party who first pursued and who were sending the dogs after them. He was put in the stocks for personal revenge, because he tried to escape. The papers he signed before he attempted to escape he did not consider a parole of honor—he did not know what he was signing.

Pitt was one of the men to aid Hogan. At peril of being put into the stocks himself, if discovered, he managed to furnish Hogan with a blanket and sundry other comforts.

When Hogan, after his capture, was brought before Captain Wirz, that dignitary assumed a very furious attitude, and made all manner of threats, but after awhile he softened down and said, in his usual tone, "Now Hogan, you sees you can't escape Captain Wirz. I prings you pack every time. Now, if I puts you not in the stocks, and parole you, will you give me your word of honor that you will not run away again?" To which Hogan replied that he would endeavor to escape "as long as he had breath in his body." This enraged Wirz to an indescribable degree. He replied: "You tam Yankee upstart, I show you what you're about. I put you in the stocks. I give you no rations. I keep you there till you die."

As is shewn in the testimony, he was placed in the stocks, and probably would have died but for the kind interposition of true friends.

Pitt was detailed on the 27th of April to service in the small-pox hospital, which was about a half mile from the pen. One day he had a personal interview with Captain Wirz, under circumstances which may seem romantic enough in narration, but at the time of their occurrence caused in his mind many painful apprehensions. His own statement of the case is as follows:

One day, as I was away some distance from the small-pox hospital, picking berries, the hounds followed my track, and, as I had no immediate way of escape, I climbed a tree. The hounds were called off, and I descended to terra firma, I did not get bit for Turner was not with them, but a couple of the 55th Georgia. I was conducted to Capt. Wirz head quarters who immediately ordered me to the stockade, but Dr. Shepperd being present interceded for me. Wirz was bound to send me to the stockade, but Dr. Shepperd protested against it, they had quite an altercation in nearly the following.

Capt. Wirz.—Take that Yank to the stockade.

Dr. Shepperd.—He went by my orders, and shall not be sent to the stockade.

Capt. W.—I command this prison, and shall send him where I tam please.

Dr. S.—I out rank you. Billy is under my charge, and shall not be sent inside.

W.—Got tam pretty Dr. you are, you takes sides with the yank, you not true to the confederacy.

Dr. S.—(turning to me) Billy go to your quarters.

The guards were standing in the doorway and I could not obey the doctors agreeable command, they talked for sometime till the doctor looking round saw me standing near him and said, Billy if you don't go to your quarters I will send you to the stockade myself, that was enough for me, guards or no guards and so I made myself scarce, no rusty looking reb could guard me any longer, I went to my shanty and thanked God on my knees for his goodness toward me and Doctor Sheppard for interceding in my behalf and preventing me from returning into the charnel house of the South. The consequence was I obtained a pass to go two miles in every direction from camp, Dr. S. was a very humane and good man to suffering men, he was in the rebel ranks at Chancellorville doing duty as a private for 15 months, and 73 years old.

CONCLUSION.

THE PAROLE—THE CAPTIVES SET FREE—DEPARTURE FROM DIXIE—HOME, SWEET HOME.

The writer has abstained as far as possible from going into the minute details of the loathsome sufferings of our prisoners at Andersonville. The pen almost refuses to record the particulars of their distressing scenes, and but few readers would like to peruse them.

It is believed that the map will fully explain itself, therefore we do not deem it necessary to go into further explanation. There had constantly been rumors of parole in circulation for a long time. but they all proved groundless, and the prisoners after a while began to place but little faith in them. Each one as it came raised some hope which was soon to be followed by sad disappointment, but on the 17th of March, 1865, the orders were ascertained to be a fixed fact. The prisoners were ordered to fall in and to their delight they found they were "home-ward bound." But here began a scene, many of the sick and emaciated could not reach the cars, others could with all their physical exertion expended manage to get there and would then fall down exhausted. Many a man was to be seen carrying his friend and comrade on his back. All had the most extreme anxiety to get started for "Home Sweet Home."

> "Who has not felt how sadly sweet
> The dream of home, the dream of home.
> Steal o'er the heart, too soon to fleet,
> When far o'er sea or land we roam?
>
> Sunlight more soft may o'er us fall,
> To greener shores our bark may come;
> But far more bright, more dear than all,
> That dream of home, that dream of home."

How intensified must have been the emotions of these poor victims as compared with those whose case is indicated in the foregoing lines. Some in their exertions to reach the cars soon expired; others died along the route.

The destination of the Western prisoners was St. Louis, which they reached by the following route: Railroad to Montgomery, Ala.; down the Alabama River to Selma, about one hundred and fifty miles; from Selma to Thermopolis; up the Tombigbee River to McDowell's Landing; then by railroad to Jackson, Miss.; from Jackson they were marched about thirty-six miles to the Big Black River; from there by rail to Camp Fisk, four miles from Vicksburg, where they camped three weeks.

At this point Mrs. Gov. Harvey visited the camp and furnished in a liberal manner writing paper, news papers, books, combs, brushes, towels, razors and all manner of little conveniences which were very highly appreciated by the men.

It is also believed that through her influence the men procured vegetables, such as onions, potatoes, &c. From Vicksburg the prisoners went by steamer to St. Louis, arriving at Benton Barracks the 24th day of April. After two weeks detention there the prisoners got furloughs for home.

Anderson was received with such hearty demonstrations when he was discovered in the cars of the road on which he had so long been employed, that some of the more timid of the passengers half suspected that the train had been siezed by guerillas.

He soon took his former position where he is now at work.

Pitt on his arrival at home was warmly welcome and received by his numerous friends, but some domestic afflictions diminished in a large degree his enjoyment on the occasion.

www.ingramcontent.com/pod-product-compliance
Lightning Source LLC
Chambersburg PA
CBHW020248090426
42735CB00010B/1864